THE PROFESSIONAL WRITERS GUIDE

Prepared by

THE NATIONAL WRITERS CLUB

Editor: Donald E. Bower
Co-editor: James Lee Young
Contributing Editor: Jim Norland

THE NATIONAL WRITERS CLUB
Aurora, Colorado

Printed in the United States of America by The National Writers Press, 1450 S. Havana, Aurora, CO 80012.

International Standard Book Number: 0-88100-065-5
Library of Congress Catalog Card Number: 89-063329

TABLE OF CONTENTS

CHAPTER   PAGE

INTRODUCTION v

THE WRITER'S CORNER vii
    The Importance of Being a Writer

1   THE TOOLS OF THE TRADE 1
    The Tools and a Test 2
    Office Equipment 4
    Supplies 7
    A Writer's Library 8
       Dictionaries
       Encyclopedias
       Periodicals
       Reference Books
       Fact Books

2   SEARCHING AND RESEARCHING 17
    Sources of Research Material 18
       Research Methods
       Libraries
       Government Agencies and Publications
       Information Networks
       How to Use Resources

    THE WRITER'S CORNER 24
    Alibis for Writers

3   WRITING AND REWRITING 27
    Getting the Idea 27
    It's Time to Write 29
    It's Time to Rewrite 29
    How to Criticize Your Own Manuscript 30
    Writing the Novel 34
    Short Story Writing 37
    Scriptwriting 38
    Writing a Column 40
    Writing Book Reviews 41
    Article Writing 43
    Poetry 44
    Editorial Services 45
    Professional Way to Prepare Your Manuscript . . . 46
    Proofreader Marks 49

THE WRITER'S CORNER 51
Finding Your Ideas

4   SELLING WHAT YOU WRITE 53
How and Where to Sell What You Write 54
Writing for the Book Market 61
The Juvenile and Young Adult Market 64
The Fantasy/Science Fiction Markets 68
The Mystery and Detective Market 71
Men's Magazines 74
Women's Magazines 76
The Confession Market 77
The Inspirational Market 80
The Educational Theatre 84
The Youth Theatre 87
Fillers and Short Articles 89
What Syndication is All About 93
Market Directories 96
How to Write a Query Letter 100

5   THE BUSINESS OF WRITING 103
Pay Schedule for Writers 104
The Freelancer's Bookkeeping System 109
Income Tax and the Writer 114

6   THE LEGAL SIDE OF WRITING 117
Highlights of the Copyright Law 117
Literary Rights 126
Analyzing Your Book Contract 131
Plagiarism and Piracy 136
Libel and the Writer 140
Using a Pen Name 142

7   ALTERNATE BOOK PUBLISHING 144

GLOSSARY 150

INDEX 151

Introduction

The Professional Writers Guide is intended to help the freelancer, both published and unpublished, with the many facets of writing. It takes you from the first step of writing to the submission of your final draft to the editor, starting with "The Tools of the Trade," describing the equipment and supplies you need for an efficient and successful writing career. This chapter explains the reference books that are available and the books you should have in your library.

The second chapter introduces you to different methods of research: interviewing, reading, observing and reasoning. Valuable information sources, such as government bureaus and national trade and professional associations are listed, plus suggestions on how to approach them when requesting material. How to find what you need for your research and how to use various reference books, directories and libraries are also included in this chapter.

Writing the manuscript is perhaps the hardest —and most important—step for most freelancers. How and where to find ideas, tips on writing the first draft, are some of the subjects covered in the chapter, "Writing and Rewriting." This chapter also provides guidelines for criticizing your own manuscript and preparing the final draft of your manuscript.

"Selling What You Write" is the ultimate challenge for writers who seek recognition and success through publication of their work. We were tempted to put this chapter before "Writing and Rewriting" since the writer should know what market s/he is planning to submit the manuscript to even as s/he is creating the idea. This chapter describes popular and specialized markets, gives pointers on how to sell to different markets, and includes an in-depth report on the book market. First-hand reports from editors tell in candid language the major reasons book manuscripts are rejected. This chapter also lists and describes the market directories of most value to writers.

"The Business of Writing" provides a formula that helps you determine how much you should obtain for your creative efforts. Sample forms to assist you in keeping records of expenditures and expenses, plus essential information required for your tax returns are included in this chapter, as well as a suggested manuscript log.

To make you aware of your rights as a writer, Chapter Six, "The Legal Side of Writing," covers highlights of the copyright law, literary rights, how to analyze a book contract, plagiarism and piracy, use of a pen name, and the dangers of libel.

● ● ● ● ● ● ● ●

The Professional Writer's Guide represents a compilation of material furnished by The National Writers Club, plus assistance and expertise from highly qualified editors and writers, as well as experts in related fields. Don Bower, director of The National Writers Club from 1974-1986, was formerly the editor of the prestigious *American West* magazine and editor-in-chief of the American West Publishing Company. He also served as executive editor of *Colorado Magazine* for five years. His writing credits include numerous books and hundreds of articles in various publications relating to the West. His column, "Don's Corner," is a regular feature of *Authorship* and "The Writer's Corner" segments appearing in this volume were adapted from his magazine columns. He is largely responsible for the information concerning style and technique, and for the introduction to Chapter Three, "Writing and Rewriting."

James Lee Young, Director of The National Writers Club, is also the editor of *Authorship*. He has written for numerous national and regional publications, is an active freelance writer/photographer with a broad background in editing and newspaper reporting.

Jim Norland, former assistant director of The National Writers Club, contributed much of the marketing information. He is an active freelance writer/photographer, has been published in over 200 magazines, and serves as a correspondent or field editor for several national business publications.

Another expert is Ernest E. Mau, author of *The Free-lance Writer's Survival Manual* and a master of marketing, with clientele ranging from manufacturing firms to word-game publishers. Much of the information on record keeping is excerpted from *The Free-lance Writer's Survival Manual*.

David A. Weinstein, a Denver attorney specializing in trademark and copyright law, entertainment and art-related matters, provided the information for "Highlights of the Copyright Law."

Other Contributors

James L. Collins   Henry Musmanno
Dian Curtis Regan   Paul A. Luers

Donald E. Bower, Editor
James Lee Young, Co-editor

The Importance of Being a Writer

"There is a need for writers who can restore to writing its powerful tradition of leadership in crisis...Today, in the absence of vital moral leadership in the official world level it is more important than ever that writers see themselves as representatives of humanity at large. For the central issue facing the world today is not the state of this nation or that nation, but the condition of man. There is no more essential or nobler task for writers—established writers, new writers, aspiring writers—than to regard themselves as spokesmen for human destiny."

So said Norman Cousins almost thirty years ago in a lecture at the University of Michigan. What he said then is just as appropriate and meaningful in today's world.

Too often we, as writers, overlook the significance of the role we have as communicators. We forget the old adage that "the pen is mightier than the sword," and neglect our responsibility as "the carriers of the fire from one camp to another," as Rex Alan Smith stated at a recent writers' workshop.

When Samuel Johnson wrote, "Nobody but a blockhead ever wrote except for money," he was being clever, perhaps, though not entirely honest. After all, it was Johnson who also wrote, "The chief glory of its people arises from its authors." The odds are slim that a freelancer will become wealthy as a result of writing, but other rewards (the glory, possibly) provide more significant compensation.

There are certain fundamental values a writer should possess if s/he believes in the importance of authorship. The writer must be honest with him/herself and with the reader. Doing one's best is one facet of this vow of honesty.

The writer must believe in what s/he is doing or abandon the project. The author's knowledge of the subject should far exceed what is included in the final draft. "The greatest part of a writer's time is spent in reading, in order to write: a man will turn over half a library to make one book." (Johnson)

Of the thousands of manuscripts I've read over the past three decades, some 90 percent were not publishable because the authors had not put forth sufficient effort to make their manuscripts the very best possible. In many cases one more 'final draft' could have spelled the difference between acceptance and rejection. Too often the author fails to become well enough acquainted with his characters and they end up as unbelievable stereotypes. One must research characters as well as scenes and settings. Inadequate research, both in fiction and nonfiction, represents a major weakness in much of the material I've read.

These are some of the factors that relate to important vs. unimportant writing, and successful vs. unsuccessful writing. Not only does the author have an obligation to him or herself to perform to the best of his/her ability, but also to the reading public. This requires that the writer learn his/her craft well and then to become a lucid, honest communicator of ideas.

"Successful writers," Stanley Vestal wrote, "are men [and women] of character—the salt of the earth."

D.E.B.

The Tools of the Trade

If you've ever tried to fix a leaky faucet or do repair work on your car you may have ended up being frustrated when you discover that you don't have the tools you need. Whether you choose to be a carpenter, an auto mechanic, a surgeon, or a dentist, it is essential to have the proper equipment. The writer, likewise, must have the right tools, supplies, and facilities to help insure his or her success in the writing profession.

You'll find, in the first chapter of *The Professional Writers Guide*, a check-off list of items that the professional writer considers essential. While it is not necessary to have all of the equipment and supplies listed, one of your goals should be the gradual acquisition of these materials.

Obviously certain items are more important than others. A good electric (self correcting) typewriter, an adequate supply of paper, an up-to-date dictionary and some kind of recent market directory are necessary from the very beginning. Additional equipment and supplies, such as a word processor, file cabinets, specialized 'word' books (a thesaurus, book of similes, slang dictionary, etc.) can come later.

Finally, you must have a quiet place to work—preferably a room that can be devoted solely to your writing activity. If this isn't possible, consider the use of a screen to separate you from the rest of the room. In any case, let others know (family and friends) that when you are in your "writing room" you are not to be disturbed.

The Tools—And a Test

These are some of the tools of the trade. Use the check-off list to determine where you are and where you need to be. If the 'no's' outnumber the 'yes's', assign priorities to obtaining some of the missing items—especially those in the essential category.

CHECK LIST

	Yes	No
A quiet place to work	___	___
A typewriter in good condition, well-maintained or a word processor and printer	___	___
Two reams of 20-lb. white bond paper or computer paper	___	___
Newsprint (or other cheap paper for first drafts)	___	___
Carbon paper (if needed)	___	___
Envelopes (#10 and 9 1/2 x 12 1/2 Kraft)	___	___
Manuscript Boxes (heavy-duty)	___	___
Postal Scale	___	___
Access to a copy machine	___	___
A good, up-to-date dictionary (less than 4 years old).	___	___
A dictionary of synonyms and antonyms	___	___
World Almanac or equivalent	___	___
A Road Atlas (current edition)	___	___
Most recent edition of Bartlett's Familiar Quotations (edition published by Little, Brown and Co. is preferred)	___	___
The Outline of History, by H. G. Wells or History of the World, by Hugh Thomas	___	___

	Yes	*No*
Texts on grammar, proper usage and style. (Preferred: The Elements of Style, by Strunk & White Write Right! by Jan Venolia)	—	—
A notebook, three-ring loose-leaf preferred	—	—
File Folders	—	—
A filing cabinet or box to hold records	—	—
Latest edition of *Writer's Market*	—	—
Subscriptions National writers' magazine	—	—
National news magazine	—	—
One large, metropolitan daily	—	—
A current library card	—	—
A minimum of eight hours per week available for writing	—	—
A serious interest in reading	—	—
An awareness of the world and people around you	—	—

OPTIONAL ITEMS

Tape Recorder

Lap top Computer

Camera

Copy Machine

Fax Machine

OFFICE EQUIPMENT

TYPEWRITERS

A typewriter is a must for a writer, even if you also have a word processor. Handwritten manuscripts are unacceptable.

A manual portable typewriter is the least expensive, costing between $75.00 and $150.00. There are some that cost even less, but generally these are difficult to use and usually require constant maintenance. The manual portable limits the writer to some extent, since it can use only one type face and one kind of ribbon. Since it is lightweight and does not require an electrical outlet it is particularly convenient if you are traveling.

The next step up is the electric portable. Most of these are reasonably priced (between $200 and $500) and are easier to use than a manual. Some electric portables offer the advantage of a choice of either cloth or carbon ribbon, and an automatic correcting feature.

The office-style (usually called 'standard') electric typewriters, such as IBM and Xerox, have correction features and the ability to change pitch (type size) and type styles. One disadvantage: they are too heavy to move around easily.

Having a typewriter that is easy to use makes an author's life more enjoyable, more productive, and less fatiguing. But one must treat this mechanical marvel with respect. Keeping dust, dirt, paper clips and such out of the integral parts of the machine, plus regular maintenance, will save expensive trips to the repair shop. And a good quality, dark ribbon (black) and clean keys will help to win points with your editor.

WORD PROCESSORS

Having a word processor is a practical dream for most authors. With the cost of word processing equipment only slightly more than an electric typewriter the dream can become a reality for the serious writer. There are many types of systems from which to choose and one should take considerable time when trying out various word processors and printers to be certain that s/he gets the system best for his/her needs.

The primary advantage of a word processor is simplifying the editing and revision process. Words, paragraphs, even pages, can be deleted or moved from one section of a manuscript to another without extensive retyping. Different software packages (software is the program that tells the word processor what to do) are available and are equally as important as the hardware (the equipment itself).

Selecting a printer carefully is important. Basically there are two types of printers: the dot matrix and the letter quality. The dot matrix prints faster, but the letters are composed of tiny dots which make reading the type a bit more difficult. More and more editors are advising that they will not accept manuscripts printed with a dot matrix printer. A letter quality printer provides type identical to that obtained from an electric typewriter and is acceptable by all editors. Many dot matrix printers do have "near letter quality" (NLQ) capability. Laser printers provide letter quality and are faster than other letter quality printers.

Letter quality printers usually print about 45 characters per second, or a full page of double-spaced copy in half a minute. The letter quality printer is also more expensive than the dot matrix. Ideally, an author who is seeking maximum production should consider using a dot matrix printer for rough drafts and a letter quality printer for final manuscript preparation.

It is possible to find dealers selling word processors who will run the disks from your machine on an in-house printer, saving the expense of purchasing a printer at the outset.

Selection of a software program especially designed for manuscript work is very important. Check with your local supplier and computer magazines to determine the program that will work best for you.

CAMERAS

A writer can frequently double sales and income with the skillful use of a camera. Today's automatic cameras, particularly the 35-mm. size with interchangeable lenses, will allow most people to take professional-quality photographs with a minimum of training. Advanced film technology brings the capabilities of taking pictures under 'natural light,' or indoors under 'low light' conditions without the necessity of using a flash.

A writer would do well to invest $150 or more in the camera body; that is, the basic mechanism including the film housing, shutter and exposure controls that operate no matter what lens is being used. While the normal or standard lens that comes with a camera is often the best bargain in an all-purpose lens, the writer-photographer should invest at the same time in a wide- angle lens (24 to 28 mm. focal length) and a moderate telephoto lens (100 to 150 mm. focal length). If you can't afford one or both of these at the outset, be sure that your basic camera can be fitted with such lenses in the future, and obtain them as soon as possible. The wide-angle and telephoto lenses give you the opportunity to present unusual breadth and perspective in your photos, to lift them above the ordinary eye-level snapshots that most amateurs take.

Take a photo class at your local high school, community college, "Y", or even at the store where you purchased the camera. Study published photographs and analyze how they were taken. Read the instruction book that came with your camera and put your camera through its paces several times before trying it in a critical situation, so that you'll know in advance how it's going to work and how to compensate for unusual situations.

Standardize on the films you use. Most photographers prefer a medium to high speed black-and-white film, such as Kodak's Plus X or Ilford's HP-4, and a slower speed color film such as Kodachrome 25, or Fujichrome 64. Except for your own family album, avoid color print film. Editors prefer and frequently demand color slides.

Don't attempt to submit instant-print photos or those taken with miniature format cameras, such as the 110 or Disk models. Editors generally require the sharpness and fidelity that a 35- mm. or larger camera delivers. Of course, if you have the only existing photo of the collapse of a major building or some such news event, any photo may be acceptable.

TAPE RECORDERS

Tape recorders are extremely useful to the writer during interviews. A recorder not only increases the data one collects but also decreases the chance for error in fact. Pocket-size recorders are now available with reproduction quality quite adequate for voice recordings. The small recorder is easy to carry around and is less obtrusive during the interview, which often puts the subject more at ease. **Be sure, however, that your subject knows you are recording and has given permission for you to do so.**

SUPPLIES

PAPER

Using a very thin or erasable bond paper for the final draft of your manuscript may be a strike against you even before the editor has read the title of your work. Use a 20-lb. bond white paper, or a 20-lb. offset paper, for your final draft. The same criteria exist if you are using computer paper. You might check with your local printers or computer store to determine if they might sell you paper at a lower price than the stationery store. Also, you might ask if they have any scrap paper that might be suitable for rough drafts.

RIBBONS

Use of a cloth ribbon is acceptable on final drafts providing it makes a dark impression and provides easy-to-read copy. Save your old cloth ribbons for your rough drafts.

Carbon ribbons provide a more professional-appearing manuscript, since the impression is always clean and even. But they are more expensive and can be used only once.

Do not use any color for ribbons other than black.

CORRECTION SUPPLIES

Manuscripts should be submitted error-free. Make any corrections neatly and unobtrusively. Avoid erasures which often leave a thin or rough spot on the paper and make it difficult to overtype the correct letter or word.

Some editors view white correction tape as an unprofessional way to correct a manuscript since the tape can peel off.

The self-correcting ribbon (now available on standard electric typewriters and many portable electrics) is the most satisfactory correcting method. When purchasing a typewriter with a self-correcting feature be sure it uses 'lift-off' tape. Some of the cheaper portables 'cover' the mistake with white-out, which can become chalky and also cause maintenance problems.

Another option is correction fluid. The fluid is placed over the mistake, thus 'erasing' it. The correct letter or word is then typed over the erased area. You must be sure that the fluid is completely dry before retyping.

Obviously these methods are not required if you are using a word processor.

A WRITER'S LIBRARY

Volumes prefixed with an (*) are recommended for your writer's library. Books marked as (O.P.) are out of print but may be available at your local library.

DICTIONARIES

A writer's tools for writing are words. The author must use the proper ones to make his writing clear. Unabridged dictionaries contain virtually all the words in the English language; however, they are revised less frequently than abridged editions. Most professional writers prefer an abridged edition, and one that has been revised in the past four years. Merely looking at the copyright date in a dictionary does not indicate when it was last revised. Normally the publisher will indicate on the copyright page when the dictionary was last revised.

UNABRIDGED DICTIONARIES:

Webster's Third New International Dictionary. One volume; 470,000 entries.

Oxford English Dictionary. Thirteen volumes; 240,000 main entries; 414,825 total words and almost two million illustrative quotations.

Random House Dictionary. One volume; 260,000 entries and 50,000 simple illustrative examples.

ABRIDGED DICTIONARIES:

American Heritage Dictionary (Houghton Mifflin). Approximately 50,000 entries. Frequent updating.

*Random House College Dictionary (Random House). 170,000 entries. 1982 ed.

Shorter Oxford English Dictionary (Oxford University Press). 202,000 entries. Not revised regularly. Last revision was in 1972.

Webster's New World Dictionary (Simon & Schuster). 160,000 entries.

*Webster's Ninth New Collegiate Dictionary (Merriam-Webster). 160,000 entries. Revised in 1983.

World Book Dictionary (World Book, Inc.). 225,000 entries. Two volumes.

SMALL DESK AND POCKET DICTIONARIES:

American Heritage Dictionary (Dell). 55,000 entries; soft cover.

Concise Oxford Dictionary of Current English (Oxford University Press). 40,000 entries; hard cover.

*Funk & Wagnalls Standard Dictionary (New American Library). 82,000 entries; soft cover.

Longman Dictionary of Contemporary English (Longman). 55,000 entries.

Merriam-Webster Dictionary (Pocket Books). 57,000 entries; soft cover.

New York Times Everyday Dictionary (Times Books). 85,000 entries; hardcover and soft cover.

Oxford American Dictionary (Oxford University Press). 70,000 entries; hardcover and soft cover.

*Random House Dictionary (Ballantine Books). 70,000 entries; paperback.

*Webster's New World Dictionary (Popular Library). 59,000 entries; paperback.

SPECIALIZED DICTIONARIES:

Dictionary of Modern English Usage (Oxford University Press). Usage manual.

March's Thesaurus and Dictionary of the English Lanuage (Abbeville Press).(O.P.)

Oxford Dictionary for Writers and Editors (Oxford University Press). Lists preferred spellings, abbreviations, punctuation and usage, identification of proper names.

Oxford Dictionary of English Etymology (Oxford University Press). Provides origin and development of words.

Synonym Finder (Rodale Press). Lists over a million synonyms for 17,000 words.

Webster's New Dictionary of Synonyms (Merriam-Webster). Carefully shows the difference between similar words.

Wood's New World Unabridged Rhyming Dictionary (Simon & Schuster).

ENCYCLOPEDIAS

When a writer needs facts and background material, s/he finds the encyclopedias a good place to obtain a concise, overall picture. The last volume of the set is the index, and refers to cross reference items on each subject. Most encyclopedias are similar in arrangement of their materials. Articles are arranged alphabetically by subject. Some of the larger sets are published by Encyclopedia Brittanica, Americana, Collier's and McGraw-Hill. The bibliographies given in encyclopedias are valuable in leading to further, more in-depth research.

The *Columbia Encyclopedia*, in one-volume, has many short, unsigned articles, illustrations limited to maps, and is a handy desk-size reference for quick use. The Lincoln Library has its material classified in twelve divisions with a full index at the end. It gives concise information, making use of many tables and charts.

For specialized interest, several encyclopedias are available. Two of them are the McGraw-Hill *Encyclopedia of Science and Technology*, and the *Encyclopedia of Philosophy* by Macmillan. Other encyclopedias specialize in medicine, law, and other professions.

While it may save considerable time and trips to the library, most writers find a complete set of encyclopedias too expensive, particularly considering that within a few years the encyclopedia is out of date. A one-volume encyclopedia is probably adequate for general use, providing it has been revised within the last four or five years.

PERIODICALS AND PERIODICAL INDEXES

No writer whose stock in trade is articles can get along without the *Readers' Guide to Periodical Literature*. The word "periodical" refers to any publication that appears at regular intervals, as monthly, weekly, or yearly. The contents of more than one hundred magazines are listed in the *Readers' Guide*. Articles are arranged alphabetically by author and subject, with the main entry appearing in bold face type at the left of the column. Abridged *Readers' Guide* is published monthly from September to May, with indexing for June, July and August included in September's issue. All entries are cumulated into a bound volume at the end of the year. Articles are listed within a few weeks after they appear in the magazines. Volumes go back to 1901. For older information, consult *Poole's Index to Periodical Literature*, which indexes contents of over twelve thousand volumes of 470 magazines published between 1802 and 1906. Excellent for first-hand accounts of wars, social customs, etc. Following are excerpts from an abridged *Readers' Guide*:

Subject entry   Dog racing
                        Foolmaster to the hounds. M Hunn and E.
                        Dickson il Pop Mech lll:140-2 Mr. '59

The entry is about dog racing. The title of the article is "Foolmaster to the Hounds" and it was written by M. Hunn and E. Dickson. It is illustrated and found in Popular Mechanics, Vol. III on pages 140-142 of the March, 1959, issue.

Author entry   Donley, Edna
                Teacher of the year por Sr. Schol
                74:6
                Ap. 17 '59

This entry was written by Edna Donley, the title is "Teacher of the Year" and the article is found in the Senior Scholastic, Vol. 74 on Page 6, of the April 17, 1959, issue.

Title entry   Doomsday and Mr. Lincoln: story
                see Horgan, P.

This is the title entry; one would have to see the author entry to try to find all the information that is needed. See P. Horgan.

For current and past newspaper articles, use the *New York Times Index*. It is published throughout the year, with annual volumes of the twice-a-month issues. The Index can be used as a guide to your local newspaper which every library is likely to keep. Major news stories are printed on the same day everywhere. The *New York Times Index* is valuable for first-hand reports of events that may have happened a half century ago or longer.

Another helpful index which covers trade and professional magazines is the Public Affairs Information Service.

REFERENCE BOOKS

(Books marked O.P. are out of print and may be available at your local library)

TERMS AND QUOTATIONS

Bartlett's Familiar Quotations (Little, Brown). When it is necessary to find the correct text and source of a quotation. Indexed by key words and first lines.

Kind Words: A Thesaurus of Euphemisms (Facts on File). Provides detailed lists of euphemisms on many subjects. (O.P.)

The Book of Jargon (Macmillan). Lists jargon and technical terms used in media, the arts, entertainment, advertising, fashion, computers, sports. (O.P.)

Dictionary of Film and Television Terms (Harper & Row).

Sports Lingo: A Dictionary of the Language of Sports (Atheneum). Covers forty sports. Helps generate story ideas.(O.P.)

The Illustrated Encyclopedia of Crossword Words (Workman Publishing). Alphabetized list of obscure puzzle answers.

Words in Action (University Press of America). Words and phrases found in today's good writing.

The Bookman's Glossary (R. R. Bowker). Terms which have been incorporated in today's language because of the many computers in use.

Abbreviations Dictionary (Elsevier). Lists abbreviations.

GRAMMAR AND USAGE

*The Elements of Style (Macmillan). One of the most comprehensive books on correct use of words.

*Write Right! (Ten Speed Press). Simplified easy-to-use grammar book.

A Dictionary of Modern English Usage (Oxford University Press).

A Manual of Style (The University of Chicago Press). Standard for the publishing industry. Covers book making, style, production, printing, editing.

A Writer's Guide: Easy Ground Rules for Successful Written English (Prentice-Hall). Presents fundamental concepts of grammar in a logical manner.

March's Thesaurus and Dictionary of the English Language (Abbeville Press). (O.P.)

SYNONYMS/ORIGIN OF WORDS

Oxford Dictionary of English Etymology (Oxford University Press). Provides origin and development of words.

Synonym Finder (Rodale Press). Lists over a million synonyms of 17,000 words.

*Webster's New Dictionary of Synonyms (Merriam-Webster). Carefully shows the difference between similar words.

*Roget's Thesaurus of English Words and Phrases (St. Martin). Valuable handbook of synonyms and near synonyms; helps you select the right word.

Webster's Collegiate Thesaurus (Merriam). Information similar to Roget's but with more simplified cross-reference.

A Second Browser's Dictionary (Harper & Row). A compilation of words and their histories. (O.P.)

One Word Leads to Another (Dembner Books). Etymology and changing meanings, pronunciations and spellings of words.

Word for Word (Verbatim Books). The history and use of related words.

POETRY/RHYMING

Wood's New World Unabridged Rhyming Dictionary (Collins Publications).

Granger's Index to Poetry (Ayers). Useful for looking up such questions as: Who is the author of a particular poem? What is the title of the poem beginning with the line....? Indexed with title and the first line of poem and both are used in connection with the author index and subject index.

Poetry Explication: A Checklist of Interpretation Since 1925 of British and American Poems Past and Present (G. K. Hall).

The Complete Rhyming Dictionary (Doubleday). Includes an excellent explanation of all the verse and stanza forms, from the limerick to the sonnet, with examples.

The Poet's Handbook (Writer's Digest Books). Covers technical side of poetry writing.

The Songwriter's Rhyming Dictionary (Facts on File). Helps the songwriter find rhyming words.

LEGAL REFERENCE BOOKS

The Protection of Literary Property (Writer). Tells everything a writer needs to know about copyright, plagiarism, libel, book contracts and gives illustrative cases. By Philip Wittenberg.

How to Register a Copyright and Protect Your Creative Work (Chas. Scribner's Sons). Explains the copyright law.

The Writer's Legal Guide by Tad Crawford (Hawthorn). 1978. A complete handbook covering copyright laws, income tax, libel, contracts, censorship, estate planning, public support.

The Writer's Legal Companion, by Brad Bunnin and Peter Beren (Addison-Wesley) 1988. How to deal with copyrights, contracts, libel, taxes, agents and publishers.

Law and the Writer, Kirk Polking, editor (Writer's Digest Books). Easy-to-understand description of the copyright law.

How to Protect Your Creative Work, by David Weinstein (John Wiley & Sons), 1987. All you need to know about copyright.

COMPUTERS

Encyclopedia of Computer Terms (Barron's Educational Series). Introduction to computerese.

Computers for Everybody (Weber Systems). The beginner's guide to computers.

FACT BOOKS

International Encyclopedia of the Social Sciences (Free Pr). Excellent reference work to find material related to history, geography, government, economics, psychology.

Encyclopedia of American History (Harper & Row). Find out what happened on any given date.

*The World Almanac. A compendium of facts, published yearly.

Webster's New Geographical Dictionary (Merriam). Location and description of all lands.

Encyclopedia of U.S. Government Benefits (Klein Publications).

Talking Tech: A Conversational Guide to Science and Technology (Morrow). (O.P.) Essays on 70 technological phenomena.

Instant Information, by Joel Makower & Alan Green (Prentice-Hall) 1987. Names and numbers of nearly 10,000 government agencies, corporations, trade associations, think tanks. Sources of expert information on more than 40,000 subjects.

AUTHORS/REFERENCES TO PUBLISHED MATERIALS

Twentieth Century Authors (Wilson). Useful reference book similar to the Kunitz series, limited to contemporary authors.

Literary History of the United States (Macmillan). (O.P.) Special volume dealing with bibliographies of American authors.

Short Story Index (Wilson). Useful for finding the name of a book that has a short story contained in it. Useful for lists and short stories on given topic or by a certain writer.

Essay and General Literature Index (Wilson). The only place to find lists of articles and essays on a given subject that are contained in books covering a range of subjects.

Dictionary of Fictional Characters (Writer). Lists 20,000 characters from more than 2,000 literary works.

Masterplots (Salem Pr).(O.P.) To get a quick summary of a plot of a novel or piece of writing.

Books in Print (R.R. Bowker). Subject, author and title. A list of all books that are still in print at the time the book is issued. These books also have a list of publishers. Helpful for a writer to research if a publisher has recently published certain subjects.

Fifteen Thousand Useful Phrases: A Practical Handbook of Pertinent Expressions (Richard West).

Book Review Digest (Wilson). A collection of volumes consisting of excerpts of book reviews. Useful for bibliographies or to make a quick estimate of the worth of the book.

MISCELLANEOUS REFERENCE WORKS

Reader's Encyclopedia (T. Y. Crowell). Useful short reference work on miscellaneous matters.

History of the English Novel (B & N Imports). The standard on the English novel.

A Guide to Greeting Card Writing (Writer's Digest Books). Provides information for writing and marketing greeting cards.

Searching and Researching

An old adage says you should write about things with which you are familiar. The logic is that whatever you write must be believable and obviously if your writing is based on personal experience or personal observation it will be more accurate than if you wrote about a place you never saw or about events you never experienced.

But if we accept this concept literally all of our books, stories, or articles would be extremely limited in scope. It is through searching and researching that we can broaden our horizons and thus expand the areas open to us as writers.

For a great many creative people the thought of doing research is distasteful and too often is ignored or at best quickly and sloppily done. One should compare doing research with building the foundation for a house. If the footings aren't deep enough or the concrete isn't allowed sufficient time to dry properly, the home itself will suffer irreparable damage.

Too many writers decide that they would rather write fiction for the very wrong reason: They won't have to do research, but can merely sit at the typewriter and create from their imagination. If you read the successful novelists it becomes obvious that many months of intensive research preceded the actual writing of their books. James Michener, for example, has the equivalent of a library full of notes for just one book—in addition to traveling to the sources and living among the people who are native to the region.

But research, like writing, requires education and training. Knowing the proper methods, the right procedures, will make your time spent as a researcher more productive and less tedious. Chapter Two will help to show you the way.

SOURCES OF RESEARCH MATERIAL

Four of the most common research methods are:

1. **Interviewing:** helpful when facts have not been put in writing and/or if you want to know more than what you have read about an incident or person.

2. **Reading:** most anything you would want to know probably has been documented. Often, the difficulty in this method is locating the right material.

3. **Observing:** extremely useful since you will be able to write from first-hand, personal experience.

4. **Reasoning:** putting together different facts for the purpose of reaching a conclusion.

THE LIBRARY—YOUR MAJOR RESOURCE CENTER

It is essential for the professional writer to be familiar with the library facilities in his own area, and also to be knowledgeable about other libraries throughout the country offering special resource material that is invaluable to the writer.

HOW TO FIND THE LIBRARY YOU NEED

Your local libraries:
> The city public libraries
> The suburban public libraries
> The county libraries
> University or college libraries
> Historical society libraries
> Corporate libraries
> Medical, legal, other professional libraries

The *American Library Directory* lists over 25,000 libraries in the United States and several thousand in Canada. The listing for each is complete enough so the researcher can decide if the library is specialized enough in his or her subject to visit or contact.

Another aid in finding the right library is *Subject Collections: a Guide to Special Book Collections in Libraries*. This reference book lists special collections of books in libraries around the country.

Directory of Special Libraries and Information Centers has more than 13,000 entries of libraries. Volume I lists entries alphabetically by subject and Volume II lists entries geographically.

USING THE GOVERNMENT FOR RESEARCH

To determine which branch of the government you should contact for research, you should refer to the *U.S. Government Organization Manual* which lists the purpose of each government agency. Another handy reference book is the *Congressional Directory* which lists Congressional Committees.

When you have determined which government agency should be able to help you, send a request for information to the Public Information Office of that agency. Should you be contacting a committee address your letter to the Clerk of that Committee.

The U.S. Government Printing Office has over 16,000 current printed titles which cover almost every field in which a government agency has taken an interest. These titles are available to the public. Check at your library to find out if it carries a GPO catalog or write to your nearest GPO office and ask to be put on their mailing list.

INFORMATION NETWORKS

Editor and Publisher Yearbook lists daily and weekly newspapers of the United States and Canada along with names of editors and officers at each newspaper. It also lists what each newspaper does as a speciality, i.e., business, art, etc. Newspapers keep clippings organized by subject or writer and are usually willing to provide a copy of these on request, although a fee may be charged.

Chambers of Commerce have information about the economic and geographical status of their areas and are very generous with printed material. Some Chambers of Commerce have different divisions, such as convention bureau, visitor's bureau, etc. Most states have the equivalent of a chamber of commerce generally located in the state capitol and operated by the state government. These agencies can be helpful if you are seeking information concerning tourism, industry or commerce on a statewide basis.

Trade associations can also be helpful and are generally quite cooperative. Almost every profession, trade, or industry has at least one such association. For listings of these refer to the *Encyclopedia of Associations* (Gale Research). The book is organized alphabetically by subjects. The *World Almanac* also lists a few trade associations. *The National Trade and Professional Associations* (Columbia) directory is another comprehensive source.

With modern technology and the use of computers, many information networks have been established, allowing the writers to tap into sources of data nationwide. Refer to the various computer publications for the names, addresses and specialties of these networking organizations.

HOW TO APPROACH ORGANIZATIONS OR PERSONS FOR INFORMATION BY LETTER

When you write a letter to an association, be factual and pleasant. Let the association know how it would be to its advantage to assist you, and advise the association director that you plan to acknowledge his assistance in your article, story, book, or whatever.

Explain as concisely as possible what you are looking for and, to avoid duplication of research, what you have gathered already. Be sure to include a self-addressed envelope and adequate postage with your request.

HOW TO CONDUCT THE INTERVIEW

Read as much background material as is available about your subject and/or interviewee. This not only appeals to the subject's ego but gives you a basis for more productive questions, and will enable you to obtain answers that have not already appeared in print.

When interviewing, listen closely for new leads. Let the interviewee speak but be sure you direct the conversation so it stays on the subject you are researching.

If you aren't recording the interview, transcribe your notes as soon as possible while the interview is fresh in your mind. If you are recording, be sure that the interviewee has given permission to be taped.

Use your common sense. Honor time limitations of the interviewee, and don't overstay your welcome. If you are unsure about the information given you in the interview, ask the interviewee to review a draft of the article.

HOW TO USE THE LIBRARY

The Card Catalog and Library Classification Systems

There is no substitute for the card catalog (or the library computer). It contains every piece of information relating to a source which may be helpful to the researcher. Still, moving through the card files and reading one card at a time, title, author, publisher, etc., is not the most exciting way to spend a day. With the introduction of the computer, considerable time can be saved by using this facility at your library. It is important that the first-time user request the librarian to run through the various functions of the computer.

Libraries use one of two classification systems: Library of Congress Classification or the Dewey Decimal Classification. Under the Library of

Congress system, 'knowledge' is divided into twenty groups. Each group is designated by a letter followed by arabic numerals and additional letters assigned to classes and subclasses. The basic groups are:

A	General Works
B	Philosophy and Religion
C	History and Auxiliary Sciences
D	Foreign History and Topography
E-F	American History
G	Geography and Anthropology
H	Social Science
J	Political Science
K	Law
L	Education
M	Music
N	Fine Arts
P	Language and Literature
Q	Science
R	Medicine
S	Agriculture
T	Technology
U	Military Science
V	Naval Science
Z	Bibliography and Library Science

The Dewey Decimal System is a few years older than the Library of Congress Classification and is named for Melvil Dewey who worked out this approach during the latter part of the nineteenth century. It has wide usage, dividing all knowledge into the main classes with nine divisions within each class. If all this sounds so complicated that one might envision climbing the walls of the library in frustration, it really is most convenient in pinpointing the class and subclass. Classes are numbered with hundreds as: 000 General Works, 300 Religion, 700 Arts, etc.

Examples of Classes and Subclasses in the Dewey Decimal Systems:

000 GENERAL WORKS
    010 Bibliography
    030 General Encyclopedias
    050 General Periodicals
    070 Newspaper Journalism

800 LITERATURE
    811 American Poetry
    813 American Fiction
    814 American Essays
    817 American Satire & Humor

700 THE ARTS	900 HISTORY
720 Architecture	910 Geographic, Travels
730 Sculpture	920 Biography
750 Painting	930 Ancient History
780 Music	970 North America

For the complete list of subclassifications refer to *Dewey Decimal Classification and Relative Index*, 18th edition, available at the library. It is helpful in determining the precise materials being sought since knowing the first three numerals and then reference to the card catalog indicates whether or not a source is relevant.

Having selected sources in the numerical categories, the indexes are the next order of business. No matter that books contain a wealth of information scattered between the covers, much is irrelevant to the specific topic the researcher is pursuing. Go through the index thoroughly, making a list of the pages which might contain materials directly related to your subject. By doing so, there is considerable time saved since referring to the list makes unnecessary returning to the index for each entry. It requires considerable time going back and forth from index to the proper page, back to the index, back to the page, and so forth.

SUGGESTED REFERENCE CARD

With reference to materials selected from sources, one of the quickest ways of becoming frustrated is to suddenly discover failure in noting the title or the author of the source from which the material has been taken. This is particularly true when it becomes necessary to return to the source at a later date, or where a word-for-word citation is used. One might recall that the book had a blue cover with silver lettering but there are many books with blue covers and silver lettering. And what about periodicals? Specific articles and pages?

You will find keeping a simple card file including details concerning your sources will be of invaluable help once you actually start your writing.

A sample 'reference card' is shown below.

Here is one suggestion: 5x8 cards, mimeographed, photocopied or printed, and containing the following:

Manuscript: _____	Topic: _____ Used:_____
Call No.: _____	Book Title:_____ Author:_____
Periodical Title:_____	Article:_____
Publisher/Date: _____	Page(s):_____ Vol. No.: _____
Who:_____	What: _____
When:_____	Where: _____
Why:_____	How: _____

Obviously, there is no hard-and-fast rule that 5x8 cards must be used, nor that the information must be in the above order. The researcher can adapt this table to fit notebook pages or any other handy method best suited for his or her needs. A record of information and sources is more important than arrangement.

A checkpoint behind the "Used" indicates whether the material has already been included in the manuscript. The "Who, What, etc.," furnishes immediate reference to the material in a few words that refer to actor, event, date, location of occurence, the situation and how it occurred, etc.

HOW TO FIND REFERENCE BOOKS IN A LIBRARY

One of the first steps to take when trying to find a reference book is asking the person at the information desk. Be as cordial as possible in order to develop a good working relationship with the librarian.

Another good step is to locate *Reference Books: A Brief Guide* (Enoch Pratt Free Library) in your library. It lists reference books and can save the researcher valuable time.

The *Readers' Guide to Periodical Literature* is one of the most comprehensive sources for finding references to subjects, events and persons. The *Readers' Guide to Periodical Literature* lists what articles were written on a certain subject, where a certain author's articles have been published and where to find those articles. This reference material dates back to 1900. It does not, however, provide a complete guide to all articles.

Subject Guide to Books in Print (R. R. Bowker) is a valuable tool for finding books for your research. The entries are listed by subject alphabetically. You should be able to find the *Subject Guide to Books in Print* in most libraries. R. R. Bowker also offers *Books in Print by Author* and *Books in Print by Title*. These reference books are issued annually.

The Reference Librarian is one of the most helpful individuals a researcher can find. However, self-help is a premium attribute attained through spending an hour or two at the local library and making a comprehensive list of that reference material which the researcher makes a part of his or her permanent file.

Additional facilities now found in most libraries include audio-visual materials, in addition to computer searches. Again, discuss with your librarian the new technologies available at your library.

THE WRITER'S CORNER

Alibis for Writers

Writers, especially some of the more successful, occasionally have a tendency when addressing a group of aspiring authors to emphasize the negative aspects of the profession, sometimes launching into tirades about the lack of feeling on the part of their editors, the slow pay, the delays in responses to their queries, the publisher's strong-armed tactics when negotiating a book contract, etc.

It makes one wonder why a sane, intelligent, rational person would decide to enter into such a field of endeavor. In the words of Dorothy Parker: "The writer's way is rough and lonely, and who would choose it while there are more gracious professions, such as cleaning out ferryboats?"

Fortunately, the majority of responsible writers recognize that this business of putting words together is one of the more fulfilling activities in life. As Anthony Trollope wrote: "There is, perhaps, no career of life so charming as that of a successful man of letters...If you like the town, live in the town, and do your work there; if you like the country, choose the country. It may be done on the top of a mountain or in the bottom of a pit...He is subject to no bonds such as those which shackle others. Who else is free from all shackles as to hours? The author may do his work at five in the morning, when he is fresh from his bed, or at three in the morning, before he goes there."

Dorothea Brande (in *Becoming a Writer*) says: "My own experience has been that there is no field where one who is in earnest about learning to do good work can make such enormous strides in so short a time." The key phrase is "one who is in earnest."

Doctors, when prescribing medication, often warn patients of 'side effects.' In a way writing has its side effects as well. While it is true that the writer can usually select his/her own hours, his/her own subject, his/her own working area, and while it is true that writing is one of the most independent of professions, the side effects are laziness, procrastination, a failure to produce.

But the one who is earnest, who looks beyond the blank sheet of paper in the typewriter to the byline on his/her story in *Redbook* or *Reader's Digest*, *Playboy* or *Cosmopolitan*, or sees his/her book reviewed in The New York Times and on the best seller list, is the one who circumvents the side effects that too often spell disaster to one's writing career.

Clive Cussler (*Raise the Titanic*) told a group of authors at a recent workshop that "fifty percent of you in this room, if you're writing a book, will never finish it. And of the fifty percent who finish it, there are probably fifty percent of that percentage who will send it out once, get a rejection and say, 'It's no good,' and put it in the closet to gather dust."

A good book idea might be, *Alibis for Writers*, which would be crammed with reasons (excuses?) why a writer cannot finish his/her story, article, book, or whatever. Some of these alibis could be:

1. Too tired after a day's work at the office.
2. Feeling a cold coming on and had better go to bed.
3. Too much housework to do.
4. Taking care of the children takes all my time and energy.
5. (As you are lying on the couch with eyes closed) I've got to think this idea through.
6. Tomorrow I'll be able to start with a clear head.
7. I need to take the typewriter in for repairs.
8. I'll start as soon as "The Cosby Show" is over.
9. I have so many problems I just can't concentrate.
10. It's a lousy idea so why waste my time writing about it.

The bottom line: a lack of earnestness, or determination, or desire. Too often we are impatient, anxious for instant success—or at least instant reward. How many more books would be finished if they could be written in a day, published the next day, and appear on the best seller list the day after that.

To those who are in earnest the rewards can be achieved. If you are persistent, you will write every day, or at least you will set aside a time for writing (even if no words flow), and sit at your typewriter, fingers on the keys, for at least an hour, in sickness and in health.

                                                        D.E.B.

NOTES

Writing and Rewriting

Any successful piece of creative writing requires three basic actions on the part of the author:

1. Getting the idea
2. Writing
3. Rewriting

This chapter will reveal some so-called secrets of the trade (actually, there are no secrets—nor shortcuts—to success). Most of the suggestions found in this chapter are used routinely by professional writers and help to pave the road to the ultimate goal—publication.

IDEAS

One of the prerequisites for a writer is an awareness of the world and the people around him. Simply being aware of your surroundings will result in an untold number of ideas unfolding for you. Unfortunately many of these ideas are elusive, not unlike a dream that escapes you in the morning.

So it is necessary to set up a file to capture these ideas permanently. If possible a standard 4-drawer letter file should be used. If this isn't possible start with a one or two-drawer portable file. Then acquire a box of file folders and some self- adhesive file folder labels, preferably color-coded—green for one subject area, red for another, and so on.

Every time you read something (or do something or remember something) you have an awareness that your idea file needs to be filled up with material. You should scan (i.e. read carefully) the daily newspaper, the Sunday supplements, the weekly news magazines, the tabloids—all with scissors in hand. Be sure to identify the clippings by the name and date of the publication. Then decide what subject classifications they fit.

Some basic subject areas you might use as a starter:

Human	Interest Politics	World Events
Local Events	Travel	The Future
How-to	Self Improvement	Western History
American History	Oddities	Unusual Characters

As you obtain more and more material it will become necessary to make sub-divisions of your basic categories. For example, under 'future' you may wish to include "Computers and Tomorrow's Life Style" as a sub-division. Under 'travel' you may add a sub-classification: "Dollars and Sense When Traveling Abroad." Your areas of interest and the ideas you assemble will determine the subject headings you need in your file.

Another excellent source for ideas is *The Reader's Guide to Periodical Literature*, available in most public libraries. This is not only a guide to what is being written for some of the more reputable magazines but also offers you a springboard for other ideas. As a side benefit, it also indicates what kind of material editors of the listed magazines are inclined to use. The writer should be aware that *The Reader's Guide* includes only selected magazines and is not a complete bibliography.

While in the library browse through the magazine section, checking the table of contents and noting titles of articles which are intriguing. Frequent visits to second-hand bookstores or magazine exchanges are also places where one may discover many treasures. Purchasing magazines second-hand is a substantial money-saver, but don't use magazines over six months old as a guide to editorial needs. (Older magazines can be usedful for article ideas, however.)

This search for ideas should not be confined to libraries, old magazines, current periodicals or yesterday's newspapers. While these are excellent sources, you should avoid the danger of paraphrasing someone else instead of truly creating. This trap can be avoided in several ways:

1. Using a different approach
2. Digging up some new, previously unpublished material to add to what has already been done.
3. Finding experts to interview.
4. Develop similar ideas, but from your own contacts and expertise.

Life is jammed with new adventures. It may seem, on the surface, that our life is routine, pretty much the same day after day. The fact is that every day, every hour, every minute, is a different scene. We are meeting new people, going to new places, thinking new thoughts. If you have an awareness you can glean ideas each time you meet someone, each time you visit a friend's house, each time you talk to a neighbor over the back fence, each time you take a walk in the park or visit a restaurant. One writer recalls stopping at the home of a friend and noticing an unusual hanging lamp, only to learn that the friend had made it out of paper cups, and consequently discovered that many other decorative items in her home were hand-made. It became the subject for a published article.

The idea doesn't have to be world-shaking, but it should have relevance, it should be timely, it should be simple. And since people are interested primarily in people, it should involve human beings. Finally, it should be a subject about which the writer has enthusiasm or strong feelings. As an important afterthought, it should have a market.

IT'S TIME TO WRITE

Once you have decided on the subject of your article (or story or book) and have completed your research, the next step is to outline the material so that you can put your thoughts on paper in some kind of order. If you are writing a novel it is sometimes easier to outline by chapters and to write a plot summary.

When writing your first draft avoid getting bogged down in details, and don't pay too much attention to grammar, spelling, repetitious words, etc., as there will be time later to correct these items. If you find that you are missing a fact, leave a blank and get the information after finishing the draft.

Allow wide margins and double or triple space your first draft, providing plenty of room for revisions and corrections. Should you be using a word processor the revision process will be easier, but nevertheless when printing your "hard copy" on the printer, allow adequate space for changes to be made on the hard copy.

IT'S TIME FOR REWRITING

One question frequently asked of successful writers is: How many times should I revise my story? And the answer is: As many times as necessary, or until you are convinced it is the very best you can do.

Your second draft should be more complete than the first, with most of the gaps filled in and most of the grammatical and spelling errors corrected. It is usually a wise idea to put the second draft away for a few days and go to work on another project. You'll be surprised at how many changes you decide to make after taking a second look a week later.

After rewriting for a third time your story should be getting close to being error-free as far as mechanical errors are concerned. Now is the time to analyze it from an editor's point of view.

You will find in this chapter a section called, "How to Criticize Your Own Manuscript." Read this carefully before attempting another draft of your material.

Once you feel your manuscript is ready for a final draft, prepare it in a professional manner. Follow the guidelines on manuscript preparation in this chapter.

If you have the patience and the time, put aside your final draft for at least a week. Then, if you have conscientiously followed the procedures outlined here, you can feel confident that the odds for success are in your favor.

HOW TO CRITICIZE YOUR OWN MANUSCRIPT

SOME FUNDAMENTALS TO REMEMBER

This section will discuss criticism of fiction, nonfiction and poetry, since each of these forms has its own characteristics. However, there are some basic yardsticks which can be applied to any writing you do.

The Physical Appearance. After you have completed all the polishing, and the finished product is before you, ready to make its maiden voyage, put it aside for two or three days. How does it look? Start with the title page: Does it start about 1/3 of the way down the page? Is it clean, easy to read, no strikeovers or xd out words? Margins adequate? Double-spaced? Is this same quality maintained throughout the typescript? After this examination, read it carefully for typographical errors, spelling, correct grammar. On this reading, try to avoid any concern for content.

An Objective Look. You have been so wrapped up in the writing of your manuscript that it is difficult to step away from it and put on a pair of editor's glasses. But it is important to be as objective as possible. Read the manuscript aloud. If you have a tape recorder, read it into the recorder and then listen to it. Make some mental comparisons with other stories you have read in the magazines you are hoping will buy your material.

Fiction

The process of self-criticism actually starts before you write the first word. You have an idea. Think about it. Is it sound, interesting, original? When writing the first draft, try to write emotionally, not mechanically. Don't get bogged down with a dictionary, thesaurus, and rules of grammar. Just let the ideas flow, as unimpeded as possible. Write as rapidly as you can. You will have the opportunity to revise later.

Plot. Once you have completed a draft, check your story for a plot. If it is intended to have a strong plot, there should be a definite problem—a human problem. The central character is faced with a conflict, is forced to make a decision or take an action that, on the surface, is difficult. The solution must be accomplished by your main character and in a way that is logical and consistent with his past behavior. A simple test of a plot: A person driven to do something; the doing becomes more difficult, followed by a satisfactory or conclusive end to the drive. If this formula does not apply to your story, you do not have a plot.

In today's market, a plot is not always necessary. There are many 'open end' stories, those that deal with an unresolved problem or simply present a 'slice-of-life.' However, you must have conflict and suspense. Otherwise there is no drama and little reader interest.

Characters. Probably the greatest single weakness in fiction is character development. Have you adequately described your heroes and villains? Does the reader know what they look like? Do they have distinguishing features, meaningful gestures, mannerisms that help the reader identify them? Are they real, and do they behave logically within the context of your story? Are they consistent?

The Setting. A story must not take place in a void. Whether it is science-fiction or a gothic romance, there must be a point of reference for the reader. This applies to both time and place. What months and years are covered by your story? Where does the action take place? Have you adequately described the setting, and are these descriptions woven into the story, not merely stuck into the action arbitrarily? Does it help to move the narrative along? As a test, write a completely factual description. Now rewrite this, selecting only those facts essential to your story development. Present this material in as interesting manner as possible. Now check this against what you have included in your story.

Style. This is the most difficult part of self-criticism, but the most important. You may have the greatest idea for a story ever conceived, but unless it is well-written the chances are it will never see printer's ink. What is style? Simply, it is the way you write, the words you use and how you put them together. How can you judge your style? One way is to select one or two paragraphs and analyze them. Have you used cliches, or stock words that have lost their exact meaning or are vague, meaningless—words such as 'nice,' 'pretty,' 'viable,' 'basic?' Do you use 'active' words that help to move the story along and that conjure up images?

Does your writing vibrate, move along with a sense of excitement, make the scenes come to life? A sentence may read: "It is a cold ride up to the mountains, and Luke didn't feel very well. There were lots of stars because night had fallen." But Thomas Wolfe wrote it this way: "The ride back into the hills with Luke was cold, dark, bleak, and desolate—the very painting of his own sick soul. Black night had come when they had reached the mountains. The stars were out, and around them the great bulk of the hills was barren, bleak, and wintry-looking."

Most complaints from editors about "over-the-transom" material is that it is trite, unimaginative, slow-moving, conventional and dull. By developing a bright, fast-moving, original style, you can convert your rejects into successes.

Other Checkpoints. Your story should have a theme, a purpose, a mood. Some stories don't have these virtues, but with them your manuscript has a better chance for acceptance.

Don't equate style with verbosity. Check the significance of the words you have used. If a word doesn't add something, delete it. Editors are quick to note and quick to reject stories which have been padded. Check every paragraph to determine if it is necessary.

Check your viewpoint. Generally, it is better to tell the story through the eyes of one character, although the viewpoint can be omniscient. Whatever the point of view, be consistent throughout.

Non-Fiction

There are various types of non-fiction, some requiring little or no research, others requiring many months of fact-finding. An article or book based on your own personal knowledge or experience, for example, needs little research. An article or book on history, a biography, a political work, etc., depends on the research and authenticity far more than on the quality of the writing.

The Non-research Work. Examine your idea critically: Is it fresh, or does it have a new twist? Study the market you are aiming for carefully. Refer to the *Readers' Guide to Periodical Literature* to be certain it hasn't already been done, or at least not done in the same way you plan to do it.

Style, a clever approach, liveliness, are all vital factors. As mentioned earlier, read it aloud or, if possible, listen to it via a tape recorder or by having someone read it to you.

If you have characters, even though they are real and not fictional, they must meet the same test—they must be adequately described, be logical and consistent, and come to life for the reader. If there are situations, these should have an emotional impact, preferably with suspense.

Briefly: Is it interesting? Does it get off to a fast start? Is it important, significant, or entertaining? If it had been written by someone else, would you enjoy reading it?

As with all works, refer to the beginning of this section to be sure you have checked the fundamentals.

The Research Work. There are essential differences between research, plagiarism, and paraphrasing. Using a particular book and condensing it into an article is not research. Usually, the more sources you use the more important your work will be and the greater its chance for success. Writers of non-fiction material frequently refer to 'primary' and 'secondary' sources. A primary source is the original source, for example, the actual copy of a diary from a pioneer on the Oregon Trail, hitherto unpublished. A secondary source would be material found in a published book, in which the author has quoted from an original document. Most non-fiction articles and a good many books are developed from secondary sources, although the researcher who can locate primary source material and use it properly will have little difficulty is selling his wares. Not all primary source material is located in the dark archives of a museum or library. If you are writing a contemporary piece, interviews with persons involved or a visit to the scene of the action can provide primary source material.

It is becoming increasingly important to sell your non-fiction article as a package, complete with graphics. The term 'graphics' is used to include photographs, color transparencies, drawings, woodcuts, paintings, etc.. If your article relates to recent events, be sure that the quality of your graphics is professional, that pictures are sharp, contrasty, well-composed. In historical articles, the same standards do not always apply, since the subject or circumstances may be of such significance that technical quality is less important. When using rare or hard to come by graphics, most editors are willing to look at photocopies, although you must be certain that you can furnish the originals should your article be accepted.

Once you have taken an overall look at the package you are preparing to send, let it age for a few days. Then examine it closely, reading it as objectively as you can. Unless you are writing an academic paper or a technical treatise, your article should have many of the same elements of interest as a fiction story. What about your opening? Does it grab the reader? Almost any article will be more interesting if it starts with an anecdote. If possible, try to build around people rather than events, even though the event may be the most important reason for the article. If possible without destroying its authenticity, attempt to dramatize your material, and include some realistic descriptions of action.

The use of dialogue helps an article come to life. A word of caution: Some publications, particularly in the field of history, do not permit dialogue unless it is authentic (testimony in a court trial, excerpts from a journal, etc.,) and will arbitrarily reject your piece if there are contrived conversations.

WRITING THE NOVEL

(Adapted from "The Elements of the Novel," by James L. Collins)

The elements of the novel are those aspects of its creation which make its effective structure quite similar to that of a modern day skyscraper. If it is not put together properly, it will never stand by itself or be of use to whose who have need for it.

PLOT

This is the framework upon which the story hangs. A plot is generally the sequence of action that progresses through the conflict of the story to the climax, ending with a resolution.

THEME

This is the point the author wishes to make, normally developing as the story progresses. Example: In a mystery novel, the protagonist and the reader may have learned the old adage that "crime does not pay." The theme, although an underlying factor in a novel, is a vital part.

ACTION

Action can range from a stroll in the park by two lovers to a fist fight in a saloon. The action of your protagonists is often used to develop his or her character as the story progresses, and should help to move the story along.

CHARACTERIZATION

The believability with which you construct your characters will often determine the salability of your novel. Characterization is the development of your main protagonist from the first page to the last page of your novel. When your characters become so credible that they could be compared with someone you or your reader actually know, then you have reached acceptable characterization.

DIALOGUE

This element is essential in the development of your main characters as well as a device for moving the story along. Dialogue can be used to bring out humor, anger, or other emotions that will let your reader know what and how your characters feel and respond to different situations. Through dialogue, your protagonist should also relay information essential to the story's outcome.

CONFLICT

Without conflict, a novel has little to hold the reader's interest. Conflict generally evolves around the obstacles standing in the way of your protagonist's goals. The five basic themes that develop conflict are:

1. Man against himself
2. Man against man
3. Man against the environment
4. Man against nature
5. Man against the machine (corporate, political, government)

POINT OF VIEW

There are four different points of view (and a combination of these) from which a story can be told.

1. First Person: limited, since the story can only be told from one point of view, and the narrator cannot read the minds of other characters, or have events happen at which he is not present. The "first-person" novel is usually more difficult to sell to a publisher.

2. Second Person: Creates a detached and sometimes nostalgic feeling. Is seldom used in novel writing and requires a special technique.

3. Third Person Major Character: Story told from the point of view of the main protagonist, seeing, hearing and feeling only those events that happen to the main character (as in the First Person point of view)

4. Third Person Omniscient: Perhaps most often used in popular novels today. This point of view makes it possible for the author to relate the perception and action of any of the characters.

NARRATIVE

The narrative portion of a novel covers the periods of time (and the setting) which are necessary to keep the reader informed as to what is going on and where between action scenes. The danger is to provide the reader with much more information, and more details than he needs or wants to have.

CLIMAX

This represents the culmination of the all of the events that have taken place in the novel, and is the most intense part of the story. Usually the climax follows a series of crises, each one more intense than the previous.

RESOLUTION

The resolution follows the climax and ties up all the loose ends. It explains the fate of your characters as well as the plot complications. The resolution (or denouement) should answer any questions the reader might still have after reading the novel.

FOR ADDITIONAL READING

The Art & Craft of Novel Writing, by Oakley Hall. (Writer's Digest Books)
Writing the Novel: From Plot to Print, by Lawrence Block. (Writer's Digest Books)
You Can Write a Novel, by Geoffrey Bocca. (Prentice-Hall)
The Craft of Writing a Novel, by Phyllis Reynolds Naylor. (The Writer)

Again, thank you.

Sincerely,

Sandra Whelchel
Executive Director

THE NATIONAL WRITERS CLUB

1450 South Havana, Suite 620, Aurora, Colorado 80012, 303/751-7844

April 13, 1992

Pat Weich
308 W. 104 St. Apt 10-A
New York, NY 10025

Dear Pat,

We appreciate your voluntary payment to the National Writers Club and want you to know that it is through such generosity as yours that we are able to continue to work on behalf of and provide services and information for writers nationally. NWC is

SHORT STORY WRITING

(Adapted from a report, "Short Story Writing," by James L. Collins)

The 'short story' is generally between 2,500 and 7,500 words in length. Any shorter and it becomes a 'short short story', and anything longer becomes a novelette or novella. More than in any other writing form, except poetry, every word must count. There is no room for lengthy passages or flowery descriptions.

Fiction, especially shorter fiction, presents ordinary people in extraordinary circumstances. Usually there is only one main character who is thrust into a serious situation and must work his way out by whatever means he has at hand. How you relate the details about the events, characters and situations that take place in your short story is called *Exposition*.

How the protagonist (main character) solves the problem is the **Plot** of your short story. Once you have disclosed the problem, you must build suspense, making the reader aware of all the difficulties, which continuously increase. This is called **Rising Action**.

In the protagonist's attempt to resolve the problem, he should become involved in a series of **Conflicts**. Obviously, a good story must have its share of conflicts to keep up the reader's interest.

Ultimately, as with a novel, the story reaches a major **Crisis**, requiring an important decision or important action on the part of the protagonist. This is the turning point, which leads to the **Climax**. The climax is the most intense part of your story, which should end the suspense and satisfy the reader. It must be logical, believable, and credible.

Following the climax is the **Resolution**, also referred to a **Falling Action**. In effect, it reveals the consequences of the protagonist's actions in solving the problem.

It is important that your short story have a **Theme**, a raison d'etre, such as "good over evil," or "crime doesn't pay." The theme should not be obvious, but merely be the end result of the development and conclusion of your story.

With a limited number of characters to work with, it is important that they be fully developed, believable heroes and heroines. Short stories especially are 'character stories.' Some short stories may be 'plotless', but they always must have strong characters with which the reader becomes emotionally involved.

FOR ADDITIONAL READING

One Great Way to Writer Short Stories, by Ben Nyberg. (Writer's Digest Books)
The Modern Short Story, by Herbert Frost Bates. (The Writer)
On Writing the Short Story, by Hallie Burnett. (Harper)

SCRIPTWRITING FOR TELEVISION AND MOTION PICTURES

(Adapted from a report by Henry Musmanno)

SYNOPSIS OR PREMISE

Sum up your story idea in one or two paragraphs. Then, tell who the protagonist is, what the main conflict is, and how the story will be resolved.

OUTLINE

The outline is used primarily in film scripting. This should be a narrative rendition of your script in four to ten pages. Camera directions are not required.

TREATMENT

The treatment is a detailed scene-by-scene rendition, in the present tense. It's sort of a short story with camera directions, usually 15 to 45 pages in length. Use camera directions sparingly.

ESSENTIALS OF DRAMATIC SCRIPTWRITING

All plays are generally divided into three acts, from the half- hour situation comedy to the full-length screenplay.

One page of script is equal to one-minute playing time for the full-length screenplay. The situation comedy script requires that dialogue be double-spaced, thus two pages of script usually equals one minute of playing time.

Script Ingredients

1. Premise	6. Character(s)
2. Protagonist	7. Conflict
3. Dialogue	8. Continuity
4. Plot	9. Climax
5. Progression	10. Conclusion

Formula

Act One should introduce your main characters, establish your dramatic premise, create the situation and lay out scenes and sequences that expand the information of your story.

Act Two: Your main character will confront obstacles and conflicts that must be resolved and overcome by your character.

Act Three: Resolution. Your provide the solution to the various crises that have led to the climax.

CHARACTERIZATION AND PLOT

To develop believable characters, prepare a complete biography of your major characters, from childhood to their present age, including their hatreds, loves, desires, talents, etc. To create conflict you must decide what your main characters want, what they are striving for. The frustrations of your protagonist are the seeds of the conflict. Create unique, memorable characters who develop during the course of the play.

The plot should stem from the main character. Events that happen must have causability or motivation, logical reasons for things to take place. The essential for any viable script is conflict. Without conflict, there is no adversity; without adversity there is no suspense; without suspense you lose your audience.

DIALOGUE

Dialogue should be crisp, realistic, and to the point. Good dialogue reveals character, forwards the plot, enhances the conflict, sets a mood.

ACTION

Action in a play logically results from the characters' personalities, desires and the rewards they seek. It is important that the protagonist's actions are consistent with his character. In your script, make sure that "actions speak louder than words."

SOME USEFUL REFERENCE BOOKS

The Screenwriters Workbook, by Syd Field (Dell).
The Complete Book of Scriptwriting, by J. Michael Straczynski (Writer's Digest Books)
The T.V. Scriptwriters Handbook, by Alfred Brenner (Writer's Digest Books)
Writing the Script, by Wells Root (Henry Holt & Co.)

WRITING A COLUMN

(Adapted from a report, "How to Write a Column," by James L. Collins)

Questions to Ask Yourself

1. Is the subject matter you intend to write about going to find an audience? Editors are seeking new authors with new, fresh ideas that have a wide appeal. Since most columns appear in newspapers with a broad circulation, the subject of your column must be of interest to a large percentage of the readership.

2. Do you have enough material to write a year's worth of columns? If you write for weekly papers, fifty columns will be required. For a biweekly publication, 100 columns will be required.

3. Have you considered the format you'll be using? The most popular formats are those of A) the narrative writer (i.e., Jack Anderson); B) the games or hobby format (i.e. Charles Goren "On Bridge"); C) the question-and-answer columns (i.e. Ann Landers); D) the catalogue columns (i.e. Jane Ciabattari, 'Bright Ideas' in *Parade*); E) the bits-and-pieces column (Lloyd Shearer's 'Intelligence Report' in *Parade*); F) How-to columns (on areas of your expertise).

4. Where are you going to get your ideas? You will find, once you start writing a column, that ideas seem to be self-perpetuating, with one idea leading to another. You will also find many ideas originate with your readers. You should be an avid reader, particularly of newspapers and news magazines. You'll often find hidden tidbits on the back pages that will offer a springboard. Spending time at your library, studying the *Reader's Guide to Periodical Literature* and similar reference works will usually provide a wealth of ideas.

WHERE AND HOW TO SELL YOUR COLUMN

The two basic ways to sell your column are: 1) Submission to national syndicates; and 2) Self-syndication. Unless you already have substantial writing credits, it may be difficult to interest a national syndicate in your work. One way to start is by self- syndication, which requires that you make all of the contacts yourself. You may find it is easier to get your columns published in some of your local weekly papers in the beginning, and subsequently contact papers in other areas.

Do not contract to sell your column to competing newspapers or magazines. Don't be surprised if you are offered only $5.00 or $10.00 for a column. This seems like an insignificant amount, but should you eventually get your column in 100 newspapers, the rewards are significant.

Be prepared for rejection. Your idea and your style must be good enough to convince an editor that he should replace another column or feature with your column.

FOR ADDITIONAL READING

How to Write and Sell a Column, by Julie Raskin & Carolyn Males. (Writer's Digest Books)

WRITING BOOK REVIEWS

A good way to build up your file of published credits is by writing book reviews. The pay is nominal, often being nothing more than contributor's copies of the publication and/or a copy of the book you have reviewed. Some of the larger newspapers and magazines may pay from $10-$25 for a review.

As with other types of writing, it is necessary to study the publication to see the particular slant the editors prefer. In some cases, the editor may want information concerning the book, and that is all. Usually book review editors expect your opinion of the book, as well as an evaluation.

If you have a particular area of expertise (western history, science fiction, biography, etc.), it's best to review books in that particular genre. It is also important to review new books, preferably titles that have not yet been released to bookstores, or are about to be released.

GETTING STARTED

Select two or three books that you feel strongly about, and write some sample reviews. Submit these to some of your local newspapers, if they have a review column, or to some of the smaller magazines with a review section. In a cover letter, explain the type of book you would like to review, and request that the editor send you a recent title for you to review on speculation.

Once you have become established with several publications, you may be able to obtain new books directly from the publisher, merely advising them that you are doing a review for such-and-such magazine or newspaper. It is an excellent way to build up your library.

DO'S AND DON'TS

Do
- Write in conversational, easy-to-read style
- Be concise and brief
- Always include title of the book, author's name, publisher, copyright date, number of pages, retail price.
- Comment on illustrations (if applicable)
- Meet the deadline
- Compare the book with similar works

Don't
- Use your review as a platform for your own ideas
- Review a book you haven't read
- Write from the book jacket copy
- Review books only of established, well-known writers
- Write a completely negative review (If it's a bad book, it probably isn't worth reviewing)
- Hestitate to give your opinion of the book

FOR ADDITIONAL READING

Writing Book Reviews, by John E. Drewry. (The Writer)
Book Reviewing, edited by Syliva Kamerman. (The Writer)
The Art of the Book Review, by Ralph Alan McCanse. (University of Wisconsin Press)

THE FUNDAMENTAL TYPES OF ARTICLES

Most novelists write what is called the 'genre' novel—which is a convenient way of categorizing his or her book (romance, detective, mainstream, science fiction, western, etc.). Likewise there are fundamental categories for nonfiction articles:

1. **The Self-Interest Article.** There is no surer way of appealing to the reader than by selecting a subject that can mean something in his/her life. Obvious examples: "How to Become a Millionaire;" "How to Raise Your Children Without Losing Your Mind," etc.. Subjects can relate to medicine, self-improvement, diet, homemaking, careers, philosophy, economics, parenthood.

2. **The General Information Article.** This is basically instructive, but hopefully entertaining as well. Subjects may relate to anything from skateboarding to national or international affairs, from hanggliding to politics at city hall.

3. **The Personality Article.** Character sketches and profiles continue to be popular for the obvious reason that they involve people. Such a piece can have as the central character an important person, someone in a unique profession, or a bus driver who did some helpful deed or has an unusual hobby. An observant author can find at least one subject every day for such an article.

4. **The Adventure-Drama Article.** Scan the daily paper. It's often surprising how much excitement exists in your own community. Stories of heroism connected with natural disasters, narrow escapes you may have had, dramatic experiences on your last vacation—all represent just the tip of the iceberg.

There are endless variations of these basic themes: travel articles, exposes, humor (which can be used in almost every article and add to its salability), inspirational, how-to, etc.

FOR ADDITIONAL READING

Writing Creative Nonfiction, by Theodore A. Rees Cheney. (Writer's Digest Books)
Basic Magazine Writing, by Barbara Kevles. (Writer's Digest Books)
Breaking Into Article Writing, by Sondra Forsyth Enos. (The Writer)

POETRY

This form is the most difficult of all to judge. In writing what one considers to be a poem, it must start out as an idea that lends itself to brevity—normally 20 or less short lines.

Check your poem for rhythm, a beat, scanning. Does your poem have a regular beat or one that constantly varies? Count the number of syllables in your first line. Are the same number employed in each succeeding line? A wide variety of word or rhythm patterns may be used, but there should be consistency.

Even in free verse, there must be a certain cadence. Read your poem aloud, emphasizing the beat. Do you stumble over some of the words? Are there unintentional rhymes or words that seem inappropriate? Atune your sense of hearing so that you are sensitive to sound and to the flow of the words.

If rhyme is a part of your pattern, the poem does not necessarily have to have end-line rhyme. Again, the pattern should be consistent. Say aloud the rhyming words, to be certain that they really rhyme. A poem needs variety in form just as much as it needs variety in word-images. If every line ends with a comma or a period, the poem may become mechanical. Enhance the appeal by running over two or three lines before coming to a complete stop.

What does your poem say? It may be about nothing more momentous than your pet kitten, but it should come to some conclusion about it. Does your poem build to a climax, or does it meander aimlessly? Has it accomplished the purpose you originally had in mind? Have you used picture-words, action-words?

Poetry is one of the most difficult art-forms, and writing poetry can be one of the most gratifying of experiences. But study the great poets, and read much about the techniques. As with any other writing, those who work at it can succeed, and those who are lazy will find it frustrating.

FOR ADDITIONAL READING

Writing Poetry, by David Kirby. (The Writer)
The Poet's Handbook, by Judson Jerome (Writer's Digest Books)

EDITORIAL SERVICES

Many kinds of professional services are available to writers, including indexing, translations, and specialized research, as well as copyediting and rewriting. Unfortunately, many firms and individuals that advertise their services are not entirely competent or reliable. It is important to obtain information about the background of the editorial service principals and, if possible, some references concerning their clients.

The writer should understand the meaning and value of the various services.

Criticism: This is an analysis of a finished piece of work, with constructive suggestions and, in some cases, marketing advice.

Counseling: General instruction concerning technique of writing, comments regarding style and talents of the author, suggestions concerning development of the material.

Content Editing: Similar to counseling, except this relates more to the overall concept of the material.

Revision and/or Rewriting: Revision is normally considered a detailed process of correcting errors in spelling and grammar, re- arranging sentences, strengthening paragraphs. Once the editor goes beyond this, it may be considered rewriting, although not changing the author's meaning.

Copy-editing: Copy-editing is the term frequently used by publishers, and although it includes revisions, the copy-editor will also verify facts, consistency (spelling of names the same throughout, etc.), as well as grammatical errors.

Collaboration: A combined effort between two or more authors. In some cases, one of the authors might have the expertise but lacks writing skills. In other cases, certain chapters might be written by one author who has knowledge in a specific area, and other chapters by a second author with different areas of knowledge. For example, if one author is an expert in the field of natural history, and another author is a professor of Western History, they might combine their talents in a book covering both natural and man- history.

Ghostwriting: The author's original ideas might be used, but the writing is done by another, with the author providing the material getting all the credit, in return for which he pays the ghostwriter for doing the writing. An example might be a family history, in which the person (perhaps a family member) with the material supplies it to a ghostwriter.

THE PROFESSIONAL WAY
TO PREPARE YOUR MANUSCRIPT

The appearance of your manuscript provides editors with their initial impression of your work. Don't prejudice them against you before they even start to read your material. Make your typescript as neat as possible. Type your final copy with a fresh black ribbon on white 20 lb. bond (8-1/2" x 11"). Corrections should be clean and few (if there are many, retype the page), and there should be no strike-overs or x'd out words.

If you are using a word processor, you should have a letter quality printer or a "near-letter-quality" printer. For your final draft, use a carbon ribbon.

A title cover page is not needed on any but book-length manuscripts. If you have a title page it should include your name, address and copyright notice in the upper left, and the title and your byline (or pen name) in the center of the page.

On the first page of your manuscript, begin your title about a third of the way down and center it. Begin the first paragraph well below your by-line. Indent the first line of each paragraph five to seven spaces. Double-space *always*.

If you want to set off a song or poem, a long quote or excerpt from another work, a letter, etc., do so by indenting another five to seven spaces. It is not necessary to put extra space (e.g., double-double-space) between the excerpt and the main text; it *is* necessary to double-space the body of the excerpt.

Leave a minimum of a one inch margin on the left and no less than a three-quarter inch margin on the right; no less than a one inch margin top and bottom. Type the same number of lines on each page (excluding page one and the first pages of chapters), and keep your character count as close as possible to the same for each line. Lines should be in the same place on each page. All this fuss may seem overly fastidious but it will impress that all-important editor and can be accomplished easily by drawing out a diagram for margins, with a straight line drawn down center-page, on a sheet of typing paper to be inserted between front sheet and carbon. This diagram should be drawn in black ink (with a black felt pen, e.g.) so that the lines can be seen through your front sheet.

Editors differ in the ways they prefer name, title and page number to be placed on top right-hand corner of the pages following the first page. Example: Doe/MS PREPARATION/3. Always number the pages consecutively, even in the case of a book with several chapters or sections. The editor is more interested in the total number of pages in the manuscript than in the number of pages of a chapter or section.

A stamped, self-addressed envelope (SASE) should accompany each submission, except in the case of book manuscripts where it is best to place the stamps unattached inside the box in which the manuscript is mailed (the manuscript may be returned in the same box). If your manuscript is less than four pages, it may be folded twice to fit a No. 10 envelope. Between four and eight, it may be folded once. Any manuscript, regardless of the number of pages, can be sent flat, but if it has more than eight, it must be mailed flat. The return envelope should be slightly smaller so as to fit the outside cover without folding. The best means of mailing a book-length manuscript is to place it in a heavy corrugated cardboard manuscript mailer.

Don't bind the manuscript in any kind of cover. Keep the pages loose. Don't staple or clip chapters or any other parts together.

A cover letter is seldom necessary, but if one is enclosed, it should be brief and have something relevant to say. If photos or other graphics are included, list these on a separate page and keep them together. Do not insert them between various pages of the manuscript. Include captions or other descriptions with the graphics. Don't put pages upside down or try any other trick to see if an editor has read your manuscript all the way through. Such amateurish procedures will only irritate him and cast you in an unfavorable light.

Use the number symbol (#) to indicate a drop-down or separation between parts of the text. Center this and do not separate it with any extra space above or below.

On brief manuscripts or fillers, make a physical word count. On longer manuscripts, make a physical count of four or five pages, obtain an average and multiply by the total number of pages. For an estimate, use 250 words per page if the type is Pica (large), or 300 words if the type is Elite. You should type only in these standard types. When words are to be italicized, *underline* them. Do not use any kind of exotic script.

If you feel there could be any doubt as to whether or not your manuscript has come to a close, you may use "End" or "The End" or a triple ###.

John Doe   (Rights offered)
1234 Main St.   (App. no. of words)
Aurora, CO 80012
Copyright 1990 John Doe

YOUR TITLE GOES HERE

By

John Doe (or Pen Name)

The appearance of your manuscript is your initial introduction to the editor. Don't prejudice him against you before he even starts to read your material. Make your typescript as neat as possible. Type your final copy with a fresh black ribbon (carbon ribbon preferable) on white 20-pound bond, 8½″ × 11″. Corrections should be made cleanly and if there are more than two or three the page should be retyped. There should be no strike-overs, xd out words or handwritten changes. If you are using a word processor, editors prefer that manuscripts be of letter quality printing, although good dot matrix (with double strike) is becoming acceptable. **Do not use a colored ribbon. Do not use colored paper.**

A title cover page is not needed on any but book length manuscripts, and should include the same information as shown here. You may wish to include your phone number along with your name in the upper left hand corner, and center the title and your by-line on the page.

(more)

PROOFREADER'S MARKS

⊙	Insert period	‖	Align vertically
⌄	Insert comma	=	Align horizontally
:/	Insert colon	⊐	Move right
;/	Insert semicolon	⊏	Move left
?	Insert question mark	⊓	Move up
V̇	Insert apostrophe	⊔	Move down
⌣ ⌣	Insert quotation marks	⊐⊏	Center
/=/	Insert hyphen	∩	Transpose(in text)
¦M	Insert em dash	*tr.*	Transpose(in margin)
¦N	Insert en dash	*sp.*	Spell out
#	Insert space	- - -	Let it stand(text)
✓✓✓	Equalize space between words(in text)	*stet*	Let it stand(margin)
eq.#	Equalize space between words(in margin)	*lc*	Lowercase(in margin)
∧	Caret--to mark exact position of error	≡	Uppercase(in text)
⊗	Broken letter	*Cap*	Uppercase(in margin)
ℐ	Delete	*C r.sc*	Set in small capitals
⊂	Close up	⎯⎯⎯	Set in italic(in text)
ℐ⌢	Delete and close up	*ital.*	Set in italic(margin)
⅄	Letterspace	⌇⌇	Set in boldface(text)
⌗	Begin new paragraph	*bf.*	Set in boldface(margin)
No ⌗	No paragraph	*w.f.*	Wrong font
		/	Used in text to show deletion or substitution

HOW TO MARK GALLEY PROOFS)— reset 8pt. Ctsc

It does not appear that the earliest printers had any method ⌒ of correcting errors before the form was on the press. The learned ~~The Learned~~ correctors of the first two centuries of printing were not proofreaders in our sense. They were rather what we should term office editors. Their labors were chiefly to see that the proof corresponded to the copy, but that the printed page was correct in its latinity-- ~~that the words were there~~, and that the sense was right. They cared but little about orthography, bad letters, or purely printers errors, and when the text seemed to them wrong they consulted fresh authorities or altered it on their own responsibility. ⌒ Good proofs, in the modern sense, were ~~im~~possible until professional readers were employed, men who had first a printer's education, and then spent many years in the correction of proof. The orthography of

English, which for the past century has undergone little change, was very fluctuating until after the publication of Johnson's Dictionary, and capitals, which have been used with considerable regularity for the past 80 years, were previously used on the ⌐miss⌐or⌐hit⌐ plan. The approach to regularity, so far as we have, may be attributed to the growth of a class of professional proofreaders, and it is to them that we owe the correctness of modern printing. More errors have been found in the Bible than in any other one work. For many generations it was frequently the case that Bibles were brought out stealthily, from fear of mental interference. They were frequently printed from imperfect texts, and were often modified to meet the views of those who published them.

THE WRITER'S CORNER

Finding Your Ideas

In going over notes from writing workshops I've attended, I noticed that one problem most writers—beginning and professional—experience is, "How to Get Started."

One obvious reason a writer has difficulty getting started is the lack of an idea—nothing to write about.

This is one of the easiest obstacles to overcome, for ideas are everywhere. Read the daily newspaper or a current news magazine and you'll discover dozens of article ideas, plots for novels or short stories.

Think about the people you know, their problems, and use your ingenuity in developing solutions—an article about friends whose son had a drug problem, or a novel revolving around the couple down the street who are involved in a sex triangle.

Studying—not merely reading—magazine articles or books provides sources for ideas and inspiration, as well as aiding in developing writing technique. Reading for recreation and reading for ideas require different approaches. If you are perusing a novel read it at least twice. Then prepare a brief synopsis of the story line, write descriptions of the main characters and analyze them. Study the organization and define the theme. Attempt to build a story along parallel lines, not imitating the author but duplicating his method and technique.

Another source of ideas is your own file. If you are like most writers you have a number of stories or articles that you have started in the past and never finished, or other works that you have submitted without success and finally discarded. Review these various projects to determine if any should be revived.

Allow your idea to gel in your mind for a period of time—perhaps a day or a week. When you feel confident that your work is firmly entrenched and you have the urgency to put it on paper, you are ready to write.

Once you have decided to start, set a definite time—next Wednesday at three o'clock, for example. Consider this to be an absolute commitment. Let nothing stand in your way.

If you find yourself facing "writer's block" (which is often just another alibi), try reading a book by one of your favorite authors and even typing out a few of the paragraphs in the book that you especially liked. Or, as I mentioned before, go back through your files and select some of your old ideas and start rewriting them. I find that a trip to the library to research an idea often inspires me to get back to the typewriter.

If you keep a daily notebook (and you should), you might re-read some of the notes you made on one of your vacations or some special occasion that was particularly enjoyable, then expand on your notes by writing a page or two about these experiences.

Should you start a project and put it aside, resolve that you will finish it, and set a time for doing so. Don't procrastinate. Persevere. Keep writing.

D.E.B.

SELLING WHAT YOU WRITE

The character of writing has greatly changed, not so much from a creative standpoint, but rather as regards marketing. Virtually every magazine today has a definite policy which determines the kind of material it wants. Even in special groups, like the religious, confessions, etc., there are individual differences. However much one may learn about a magazine's requirements from market tips, there is no substitute for an actual reading of the magazine itself.

Some markets are wide-open for the submissions of freelance writers, others afford only a limited market, and some are completely closed to unsolicited material. Once every magazine welcomed unsolicited material, but with the increase in population and a natural increase in the number of persons trying to write, many editorial offices are swamped with material, necessitating either augmented editorial staffs, or delayed reports on manuscripts that sometimes run into months. Writers themselves can help remedy this situation by more intelligent and conscientious marketing of their material. If the free and unhampered contact between editors and writers is to be maintained, knowledgeable marketing is virtually necessary.

In this chapter, you will find an overview of markets for fiction, articles, radio & TV plus in-depth reports on specific markets such as the men's magazine market, the religious market, the confession market, etc.

HOW AND WHERE TO SELL WHAT YOU WRITE

What Has Happened To Fiction

Many gloomy predictions have been made about the demise of magazine fiction. While it is true that many markets have dried up, there remains a steady and persistent market for fiction. The great difference today is that many stories must be specialized in order to be salable. It is now likely that if a story does not sell to a logical market, there may not be another one unless drastic revisions are made. This is a fact of life which must be taken into consideration by the fiction writer.

The Competitive Market

Obviously those magazines that pay the highest rates attract the skilled professional and are most alluring. These are such magazines as *Cosmopolitan*, *Redbook*, *Esquire*, *Playboy* and *McCall's*. Though there is a chance that the freelance writer may sell to any one of these magazines, the percentage of acceptances is discouragingly small.

The quality markets (including the various quarterlies usually issued through or by universities) such as *Atlantic* and *Harper's*, also attract the experienced professional. They are more open to the freelance writer than are the slicks, but the competition is very little less.

The Wide-Open Markets

Prolific users of fiction are the juvenile, religious, science fiction and fantasy, confessions and literary magazines. For the most part, these depend largely upon unsolicited freelance submissions for their fiction. These are the markets in which writers may gain their published credits and sharpen their skill. However, none of these magazines will accept poorly prepared or amateurish stories.

The larger number of the juvenile magazines are published by religious orders and consequently it is necessary to understand the religious principles that may be a prime consideration. This is even more true of the adult religious magazines which, for the most part, are published to further the tenets of a particular faith as well as to entertain through fiction. There is even some possibility that a story for children which fails to sell to one market may sell to another without revisions if the story does not violate general religious principles.

Almost all confession magazines depend largely on unsolicited freelance submissions. Obviously, the writer must understand the purpose of these magazines; basically, it is the act of confessing that distinguishes these stories from other types. Editors are most encouraging toward freelance writers. The confession market is discussed later in this chapter.

The literary magazines offer a wide and varied market, though for the most part payment is low or non-existent. Nevertheless, these magazines offer an excellent training ground, especially for those writers of promising creative talent; many successful novelists and short story writers found in the 'little' magazines their first encouragement. Any publication is meaningful to the freelance writer, and in this particular area, competition is for the most part with other writers of the same caliber.

The men's magazines (including science fiction and fantasy) provide a prolific market for fiction and near-fiction (stories based on truth). A good deal of buying is from freelance writers. There is much diversity among these magazines, so hit and miss marketing is usually unproductive. The men's magazine market is discussed later in this chapter.

Pinpointing The Article Market

So extensive is the market for articles that almost any kind can be sold if it is written in an interesting manner and does not deal with trite material. This market is even more specialized than the fiction market, so knowledgeable marketing is absolutely essential. The types of markets loosely fall into seven different categories. The main requirement in most instances is authoritative information derived either from personal experience or through extensive research and interviews. On the other hand, the market for essays and editorials is extremely limited except for humor which bridges all markets and is universally desired when it is in harmony with the general policy of any given magazine.

The General Market

The slicks, women's magazines, men's magazines, and other consumer magazines usually devote the maximum space to articles. Almost invariably these are written by highly experienced writers and in some instances on assignment. A few magazines will buy ideas for articles, which then are assigned to staff writers. The freelance writer can sell to this market, but his work must be comparable, in style, execution and comprehensiveness, to compete with that of established writers.

The Opinion Magazines

Publications like *U.S. News & World Report, Time, New Republic* and *Nation* offer a market only to those who are able to draw on their own meaningful experience or skillful interviews with authorities or political figures or upon scholarly and thorough research. This is no market for the armchair philosopher or economist. The university quarterlies, such as *Yale Review*, *Chicago Review*, *Kenyon Review*, *Southwest Review*, etc., as well as *Atlantic* and *Harper's*, use thoughtful or significant articles, but here too it is the exceptional writer, equipped with both writing talent and sound information, who is favored with acceptances. The freelance writer must be able to compete on equal terms.

The Specialized Markets

Various categories come under this division, such as the sports magazines, animal, western, military, regional and travel magazines. Most of these offer a reasonably good market for freelance submissions, for a fair percentage of the material used is based upon personal experience that need not be highly unusual or stemming from an authoritative source. Each classification clearly indicates the general subject matter, though every magazine has its own requirements which can be understood best only by a careful reading of the publications.

The Technical Magazines

These periodicals, such as those covering business, music, garden and home, health, science, automotive and aviation, are a very receptive market to freelance writers who know their subject. Obviously, one cannot write about technical subjects without a thorough working knowledge of them. Occasionally, a personal experience article is bought by these magazines if it has something to say to professionals.

The Inspirational and Religious Magazines

This market favors unsolicited freelance material, but articles must be well written and have something fresh to say. Virtually any subject may be discussed, provided it is researched and carefully thought out. Preaching is not favored nor is overt moralizing. It is vitally necessary to write in harmony with the particular denominational attitude of the magazine. Writers who are aware of various religious tenets may write for magazines of all creeds, for it is not the author's own religion but the ability to write in harmony with that of a given magazine that is important.

The juvenile magazines are breaking away from a strict parochial limitation; many are dealing with current problems, such as racism, demonstrations, and permissiveness. However, all kinds of non-fiction are used: articles, inspirational essays, short humor, jokes, puzzles, Bible quizzes, and various other fillers.

The Trade Magazines and House Organs

Trade journals have long been considered to be an easy way for the aspiring writer to obtain his/her first published credits. Trade publications today, however, have been steadily upgrading the quality of their articles and they are insistent upon accurate and practical information derived either from extensive personal experience or through skilled interviews.

The writer who is determined to make good in this field and is conscientious has a good chance. Editors are not only willing but eager to work with writers on whom they can fully depend. The freelancer must understand that s/he will be required to go into the field to study an industry and obtain essential facts and to interview key personnel. It is virtually impossible to sell an article to a trade paper if it is based solely on observation or personal opinion.

There are more than 600 house organs (or company magazines); most of them will consider freelance material. Generally, editors of these publications prefer to be queried before a manuscript is submitted. Payment ranges from $25 for an article to $800. In some instances reports are slow because not all house organs have full-time staffs. A few use fiction, humor and fillers.

Poetry

Every conceivable form of poem may be salable. There are literary magazines that cater to the far-out, experimental and off-beat poet as well as those that look for sentimental poems written in rigidly conformist style. The 'little' magazines offer a prolific market, though all too often payment is made in copies of the magazines. Getting published is, perhaps, even more vital to the poet than the prose writer, for if his/her work is used frequently, in any kind of medium, his/her chances of being bought by the paying magazines increase and there is also a greater possibility of obtaining publication of a volume of poetry.

Among the most prolific markets that pay for poems, usually limited to orthodox forms and conventional themes, are the juvenile and religious magazines.

Many newspapers throughout the country, even small weeklies, occasionally will print a poem if it has a strong local interest, though rarely is any payment made for it. Except for the metropolitan newspapers, local interest often transcends any particular consideration of technical merit.

The Opportunities for Book Publication

Dramatic changes have occurred in the field of book publishing in the last few years. It has become extremely difficult for the 'new' writer to get a hardbound novel published, primarily because production costs have risen tremendously and publishers are hesitant about taking a chance on a first novel. Fifteen years ago the unit cost for the average hardbound book was $2.00 to $3.00 if printed in 5,000 quantities, making the publisher's investment $10,000 or $15,000. Today, the unit cost ranges from $6.00 to $8.00, so that its investment becomes $30,000 to $40,000, and publishers hesitate to take that risk on an unknown quantity.

However, on the optimistic side is the fantastic increase in paperback publishing, opening up dozens of new markets for the first-time novelist. Many of the hardbound publishers are now publishing paperbacks also, often simultaneously with the hardbound edition. While many paperbacks are reprints, more and more publishers are printing paperback first editions.

There are still many good markets for non-fiction books, since the risk is not as great and hardbound publishers are more willing to venture capital on a new author if s/he has a sound idea and the necessary credentials to do a non-fiction book, particularly in the fields of history, biography, and how-to.

The non-fiction paperback market is also flourishing, specifically for how-to, health, physical and mental well-being books.

Children's books, if designed for a particular age group, are very much in demand. A considerable amount of originality and ingenuity is necessary here, and illustrated books are more salable, especially for the younger age group.

It is important to study the book market just as intently and carefully as one studies the magazine market. Become aware of the best seller lists, and before submitting a book to a particular publisher, obtain its latest book list or catalog and study the things it is currently publishing. Don't hesitate to ask booksellers for information about publishers and books they feel are marketable. Your librarian can also help provide information about marketing and publishers.

A Word of Warning

Despite alluring promises by so-called vanity publishers, publication by any except recognized trade publishers almost invariably results in disappointment and financial loss. Only those writers who can sell their book after it is printed should undertake a project of this kind unless, indeed, the main reason for having a book printed is the egotistical satisfaction. One of the alternatives that is growing in popularity is the self- published book, which is far less costly than a vanity published book and has a greater acceptance with bookstores and libraries.

Over the Rainbow to Television

For some time after the advent of television, those who had courses or books on the subject shouted about the great opportunity in television and the greedy demand for even more material. Unfortunately, this balloon was filled with hot air and soon was pricked. There is very little opportunity for the freelance writer to sell a script to television. Virtually all studios will consider material only if it comes to them through a recognized agent. Even then, the chance of making a one-shot sale is limited.

The opportunities in television are largely for those who have an established reputation. Those who live in the producing centers where they can work with the studio's staff have an advantage.

There is still some opportunity to sell TV rights to published short stories and novels. Most writers who hit with an occasional story are those who sell TV rights to published material. Alert writers will seek an opportunity to write for a local television station, thus gaining practical experience which may lead to a steady job or an enlarged opportunity.

Cable TV presents a relatively new market growing in popularity. It would behoove the freelancer to contact the various cable networks and local outlets to determine their requirements.

Other markets available resulting from the new technology are audio and visual cassettes prepared for consumers and corporations.

Radio—Dead But Not Buried

What once was a versatile entertainment medium, now as everyone knows is confined almost entirely to news reports, music—and commercials! A writer still may find some place in radio if he can come up with an unusual and appealing idea. The advertising arena offers some opportunity, especially if one is able to write a catchy rhyme set to a tuneful melody.

What About the Movies?

The time when the moving picture studios considered freelance submissions is almost dimmed in memory. Today no major studio will consider an unsolicited manuscript. Only when it comes from a recognized agent is a manuscript given consideration. The movies still buy rights to a good many novels, stage plays and magazine fiction. This represents virtually the only way the writer can break into the movies. At one time many an author wrote his novel with an eye to the movies, tailoring his story so that its chances of being bought by a studio were increased. The variety and inclusiveness of moving picture production today precludes specialization, for almost any type of story, even those once considered completely beyond consideration by the movies, are now bought and produced.

Stage Plays, the Broadway Touch

It is extremely difficult to sell a play for Broadway production; the market can be considered to be virtually closed to the freelance writer. Some original stage plays are sold by agents, but the number is exceedingly small.

The opportunity for New York production has been increased by the off-Broadway plays in smaller theaters and away from the high cost of Broadway production.

The best opportunity for the ambitious playwright is to write for summer theaters, local theatrical groups, the educational theatre, and to enter play contests. The latter often include a production of the play as well as a cash prize. Any kind of actual production may come to the attention of play producers who are seeking material for Broadway. As anyone should realize, the stage is a highly specialized medium and it is seldom possible for a writer to create a play unless he has some knowledge of the theater. Amateur or civic theaters provide the best chance to gain experience.

Sing Me a Song

The most alluring songs about the opportunities in song writing come from the racketeers. The hard fact is that the song publishers almost without exception will not consider unsolicited freelance lyrics or songs. Any song service or so-called song publisher who asks for money is, at the least suspect, and will do little for the aspiring songwriter except deplete his or her bank account.

In order to get a song published legitimately, it is usually necessary for the songwriter to induce bands to play his song, professional singers to sing it, and disc jockeys to play a recording of it. None of these avenues is wide open to the songwriter and entry to them is gained only through aggressive and persistent effort.

NO MARKET ACTUALLY IS CLOSED

The most tightly closed gate to any medium readily gives way when assaulted by a genuine talent. Very often ability must be supplemented by intelligent marketing and grueling persistence. The encouraging fact is that any sign reading "Closed—This Means You" is meant to scare off only the hackneyed, incompetent and those of average ability. Actually, the gate is not locked when the truly talented writer attempts to open it.

WRITING FOR THE BOOK MARKET

Perhaps the most challenging, the most rewarding, and also the most discouraging and most frustrating area of literary endeavor is book writing. It has been estimated that more than 500,000 first novels are started each year, and of these 100,000 are eventually completed. Less than one percent are ever published, and of these first novels the average sale is less than 5,000 copies. Royalties seldom amount to more than $5,000.

Considering that a book manuscript may take from one to five years to complete, an author could do much better financially in almost any other field of writing—unless his or her book is the one in ten thousand that makes it to the best seller list, or is taken by a book club, a mass paperback house, a major Hollywood studio or TV network.

As depressing as these statistics may appear, they are not intended to discourage those who feel the vital need to create a book. Contradictory as it seems, book publishers are hungry for new writers, for that unknown man or woman banging away at the typewriter in the kitchen or a corner of the bedroom of some modest midwestern home, hoping to become another Steinbeck or Hemingway, or Louis L'Amour or Janet Dailey. It is a euphemism in the publishing world that even the greatest authors were at one time unpublished writers.

What is happening in the publishing field today and what is the outlook for tomorrow? After all, if you are going to spend the next year or more writing a book, it makes sense to produce a manuscript that will meet the needs of the publisher (and hopefully the reading public as well).

Currently in the fiction field the mystery/spy/suspense novels are leading other category books in popularity, although there is a trend away from the genre novel. The contemporary romance novel no longer enjoys its number one spot, with more emphasis being placed on the historical romance.

Other genre novels which seem to hold their own over the years are science fiction, the Western, and historical novels. More emphasis is being placed on the mainstream novel, especially those with an environmental or sociological message. Among men action/adventure remains popular, with science fiction a close second. Horror and fantasy books are down the list but are categories that will remain as a permanent part of the bookstores' stock in trade.

According to a *Publisher's Weekly* survey, the sale of fiction outnumbers nonfiction books by a small percentage. The sale of historical nonfiction ranks as a substantial favorite with male readers, but biography and autobiography are the leaders among women.

Self-improvement books, such as those dealing with health, exercise, beauty care and diet, etc., continue to be in demand, particularly by women. Books relating to money management, budget, and economics are preferred by more men than women. How- to books have lost some of their popularity among publishers, although writers with expertise in a particular area can usually find a market.

The market for children's books has been increasing over the past several years, now accounting for almost 15 percent of the fiction market.

Reader interest in books concerning computers and the computer industry remains strong, though somewhat weaker than a few years ago.

The paperback publishers still remain as the best possible markets for fiction, publishing approximately 3,000 novels compared to some 2,000 titles from the hardcover houses.

The National Writers Club surveyed a dozen of the leading publishers to determine what the editors are buying, what they are not buying, and some of the primary reasons that manuscripts are rejected.

- The editors at Price Stern Sloan, Inc., consider that children's books, and humor books as currently the most important in their publishing program.
- Likewise, Longmeadow Press is seeking children's books, as well as self-help manuscripts.
- Harper & Row editors are interested in broad areas of fiction (contemporary, adventure, historical, mystery/detective), and likewise in nonfiction (biography, history, current affairs, true crime, cookbooks). "In the last several years we have virtually stopped publishing craft and instructional how-to books."
- Thomas Bourgey and Company is looking for contemporary romances and Westerns.
- The editor at NAL Books sees a decline of category fiction and an increase in gift books, and states that they are primarily interested in maintream novels and true crime books.
- The Leisure Books editor advises that "Horror books are way down; historical romances are holding steady."

WHY BOOK MANUSCRIPTS ARE REJECTED

We asked a number of book editors to tell us the most common reasons for rejecting unsolicited manuscripts, and here are some of the answers:

- "Too similar to books already in the marketplace—usually too similar to books on our list."

- "An insufficient market for the material offered."

- "Poor writing, lackluster thinking, lack of potential salability."

- "Manuscript deals with subject matter that has been flooded, or is a dead subject area."

- "Incompetent writing."

- "Not suitable for our list."

- "Do not fit our market. Also, non-writers who think they can write."

HOW TO IMPROVE YOUR CHANCES

Decide on your goals. Are you interested in writing novels, children's stories, plays, biography, how-to books, travel, history, romances?   Set an objective that is attainable. There is far less competition in the nonfiction market and this is probably a more reachable goal than attempting a novel as your first effort.

Study the Market. Editorial policies vary just as much in the book field as in the magazine field. Before deciding on the book you wish to write, obtain copies of the publishers' catalogs to see the general areas in which they are concentrating and read some of the recent books they have published. Check in your bookstore to see which books are most prominently displayed. Obtain copies of *Publisher's Weekly* from your library and study the publishers' advertisements and read the reviews in the Forecasts section to determine where the primary interest lies.

Be Professional. You must remember that you are competing with the most successful authors in the world and unless your work is 'just as good' or 'better,' you will end up with a frustrating stack of rejection slips.

Whether you are writing fiction or nonfiction, you must research diligently, carefully, endlessly. You must revise and revise and revise until you are convinced that your manuscript is the very best you have in you. And then be sure that your presentation is neat, without strikeovers, without spelling or grammatical errors, on a good bond paper with adequate margins.

Concentrate on the Query. As an editor at Bantam told the registrants at an NWC Workshop: "You may have spent eight months on the manuscript and then you dash off in three minutes a query letter that can make the difference between acceptance and rejection...Give it a lot of thought and time."

Don't give up. Unless you complete your book, you have reduced your chances of publication to zero. Clive Cussler (*Raise the Titanic*) once said that fifty percent of the people who start books never finish them, and of that fifty percent half send their work to one or two publishers and then put them away in the trunk. So resolve to complete your book, and then resolve to keep submitting it until you've exhausted the list of publishers. And then start over.

THE JUVENILE AND YOUNG ADULT MARKET

(Adapted from Reports by Dian Curtis Regan)

Should you be writing for juveniles? Writing for children is a challenge and a responsibility—a chance to change lives. Each generation grows up, leaves childish interests behind, but there's a new crop eager to learn the same things.

Though some people think the juvenile field is easy, this is not necessarily true. To be successful requires intensive study of material currently being published, as well as a special talent—a gift of using the perfect word, of being able to project oneself into the child's world.

After a temporary lapse in the children's book market, created when the baby boomers grew up, there is a renewed interest, as the baby boomers now have children of their own. More publishers are now specializing in this market, and those already in the field are increasing the number of titles they are issuing.

In the past five years, sales to libraries have increased 60 percent, and sales to bookstores have increased 200 percent! This trend is expected to continue through the 1990's.

One new trend in children's books is the issue of social responsibility. Many editors are now in favor of authors adding their own points of view instead of remaining neutral. Young readers today require realism in the books they read.

Author Katherine Paterson says, "We writers constantly disappoint parents because we allow our characters to do all manner of reprehensible things. But *telling a story* is different from *teaching a lesson*. The writer is . . inside [the characters], not outside judging them."

One children's book editor notes, "Freelance people should spend time in the children's room of their local public library in order to become acquainted with the field. Most of the submissions we receive are badly written and trite—half the time they are not real stories and lack substance. Also, writers should realize stories for children should not be pieces of propaganda."

Middle Grade Novels

Aimed at 8-12 year olds, these are in high demand. Books should be approximately 100 manuscript pages in length, full of action and dialogue, with an uncomplicated plot. Editors want to see adventure/suspense, mysteries, horse stories, sports themes and humor. Series books are especially in demand.

Young Adult Fiction

Currently in a slump, due to the endless series of books launched to compete with the popular Sweet Valley High. Single title originals are difficult to sell unless you are an established author. Topics of particular interest: sports, world situations, high school activities, romance. Some of these also apply to nonfiction.

Young Adult Series Books

Series books generally are created by packagers who edit the books for a publisher. In most cases, the author's name does not appear on the book and the work is contracted for a flat fee.

Young Adult Nonfiction

Informative books on subjects of particular interest to teenagers, such as careers, job interviews, relationships, problems, and how-to books are also increasingly popular.

OTHER TYPES OF CHILDREN'S BOOKS

Toddler Books have increased in popularity, due to the trend toward earlier childhood education. Books should be aimed at 2 to 3 year olds, and usually teach the child something about himself.

Fables or Folk Tales are mystical, lending themselves to lavish illustrations. Retold folk tales have been overdone, but a market still exists for original folk tales or fables.

Poetry Books: Themes center around school, animals, friends, and nature, and are more popular in the institutional market than in bookstores.

Easy-to-Read Books, both fiction and nonfiction, have resurged in popularity. Stories should be written at a first or second grade reading level. Controlled vocabulary lists are found in the appendix of some books, or can be requested from the publisher.

Novelty Books include pop-ups, sticker books, books that can be zipped, buttoned, or snapped, bathtub books, puzzle and activity books, and books with cassettes, stuffed toys, or TV tie-ins.

A TEN POINT CHECK LIST

1. Have you created a memorable character who is believable?
2. Is the plot fast moving? Is the story line easy to follow?
3. Is your style one that will retain interest and emotional appeal?
4. Are the dialogue and vocabulary appropriate to the age level of the characters?
5. Does the opening captivate the reader's attention and thrust the main character into conflict?
6. Does the main character solve the conflict? Is the viewpoint consistent?
7. Would children enjoy reading it, or having it read to them?
8. Is the manuscript neat, with no grammatical, spelling, or other errors?
9. Is the idea original, or a new slant?
10. Does the title fit the story? Is it original? Does it grab the reader?

It's especially important in this market to study the publications and to obtain a copy of editorial guidelines. This is one of the best places for the beginning writer, but professionalism is required, regardless of the age level for which you are writing.

RESULTS OF A SURVEY OF 50 CHILDREN'S BOOK EDITORS

NOTE: This survey was confined to editors of "illustrated children's books," general age level of 2-8.

"Do you consider unsolicited freelance material?" All editors replied "Yes," except one who did not answer. Likewise, only one replied that freelance submissions are "never of value." Eighty percent find they are "sometimes" of value, and 16 percent consider them a "valuable source."

Since this survey concerned illustrated books, we asked editors if they preferred the author to submit illustrations with the manuscript. Only two said "Yes." Four said "either," but the editors indicated they wanted illustrations only if they were professionally done. All others said they did *not* want illustrations.

The primary reasons for manuscript rejections were, in order of significance:

Lack of originality	80%
Dull, pedestrian writing	72%
Doesn't meet requirements	52%
Non-professional writing	52%
Unimportant idea	40%
Not written at proper level	24%

We asked editors to advise us of the areas they would consider most acceptable, and the majority were fairly general, stating, for example, "any original work that would engage the interest of 4-8 year old readers." However, some specific answers were obtained. Books about animals were mentioned most frequently, followed closely by adventure stories. Other categories mentioned: famous characters, humor, wildlife, science, people, how-to, mystery, heroes, crafts, realistic contemporary fiction.

A look at recent publishers' catalogs indicates a trend toward books written and illustrated by the same person, often an established illustrator. Ordinarily, royalties are split 50-50 between writer and illustrator.

If your talent is in art and you know you can do a good job illustrating a children's book, how do you get the attention of a publisher?

Do not write a children's book and illustrate it. You would do much better to query several publishers; tell them you want to illustrate a children's book. If interested, they will send you their guidelines and requirements. In all likelihood you will be asked to send them samples for their files.

FOR ADDITIONAL READING

How to Write & Illustrate Children's Books, edited by Tred Pelkey Bicknell & Felicity Trotman. (Writer's Digest Books)

The Children's Picture Book: How to Write It, How to Sell It, by Ellen E. M. Roberts. (Writer's Digest Books)

Writing Juvenile Stories and Novels, by Phyllis A. Whitney. (The Writer)

The Way to Write for Children, by Joan Aiken. (St. Martin's)

THE FANTASY/SCIENCE FICTION MARKETS

Fantasy/Science fiction—or 'speculative fiction,' as writers prefer to call it—is more popular than ever. Though the heyday of the space opera and the clash of superheroes with slimy aliens has taken something of a back seat, escape stories still sell well and will continue to do so. Likewise, preoccupation with gadgetry and technology remain an important part of the contemporary science fiction story. Where fantasy is concerned, the hardware is virtually nonexistent, though it is sometimes difficult to separate the fantasy from the SF in some stories, or vice versa.

The emphasis, especially in science fiction, has shifted to a large degree to social, psychological, environmental, historical or political problems and often nowadays SF will criticize technology, its excesses, its dehumanizing effects, rather than extol or deify it as it often did in the past. There has been a shift, as well, from preoccupation with other worlds, with evil 'out there' (though, again, other worlds and outer space remain apt territory), to a concern with evil here on Earth, or an evil that is sometimes nameless and imminent, residing in the secret heart of things.

Perhaps the biggest change in both genres is the growing number of serious, experimental and speculative stories dealing with ideas per se, with the imaginative exploration of alternate worlds and alternate realities. In other words, SF and fantasy continue to fragment, branch and grow in scope, depth and sophistication. Even as this is written, there are no doubt new unpredictable trends on the way. Be that as it may, a writer who wishes to work within this ever-widening purview must keep up with trends and learn to anticipate or initiate his or her own. No other literary genres or sub-genres rely so heavily on the new, the different, the strange. A writer in these areas should know what has been done, or done to death, and be constantly working to create fresh material. *One must know the market.* One must read SF and/or fantasy avidly if s/he wants to write it—and sell it.

A Good Market For Freelancers

Science fiction and fantasy provide one of the largest of fiction markets. Magazines strictly devoted to these fields are primarily interested in buying fiction and, while they will naturally be more likely to buy stories from established names, editors are always looking for new writers and they use between ninety to one hundred percent freelance material in each issue. In addition to the hardcore SF and fantasy magazines, there are other markets as well. Nearly all the men's magazines will buy SF or fantasy. Playboy Press has published many collections of SF stories originally published in *Playboy* over the years and *Penthouse* often runs a science fiction story (it was *Penthouse* publisher Bob Guccione who launched *Omni* in 1978). Then there are a number of SF and fantasy anthologies published each year which buy original stories. Some of these are one-shot endeavors but several have been recurring with new material annually for years. These anthologies pay on a par with the SF and fantasy magazines. For the amateur, the beginner, or the writer trying to enter these more professional markets, there are an unknown number of little 'fanzines' or 'semiprozines' published around the country. They rarely, if ever, pay anything, but offer a good way for the aspiring SF writer to learn and break into print.

As far as the freelance fiction writer is concerned, this continually expanding market can only be good news. But it apparently cannot be said enough that no genre exists that is more sensitive to the cliche because no genre exists that is more dependent on the unexplored. The most common lament among editors is that over half the material they receive from freelancers deals with concepts that went out with the forties and fifties. The most common rule is that one already referred to previously: you must read and know SF (and fantasy) before you can write it.

While Edward Bryant, a prolific SF writer and editor of anthologies, says that "none of the editors of established pro magazines are prejudiced against new writers," he and other science fiction editors bemoan the amount of trite, overworked ideas, unbelievable plots, and dull pedestrian writing they incur from unsolicited submissions.

COMMENTS FROM EDITORS

"If you're not familiar with what's been written, and with what's being written in the field, don't try to write SF." This is from an editor who is after "serious writers who have not yet made their first sale."

From the editor of *Aboriginal Science Fiction:* "Stories that will make unique use of the latest scientific theories and discoveries, have lively, convincing characters, an ingenious plot, a powerful and integrated theme and with an imaginative ending."

From *Isaac Asimov's Science Fiction Magazine:* "We're looking for character-oriented stories, those in which the characters, rather than the science, provide the main focus...Fantasy is fine, but no Sword & Sorcery or cute little elves, trolls, or dragons...A good overview would be to consider that all fiction is written to examine or illuminate some aspect of human existence, but that in science fiction the backdrop you work against is the size of the universe."

The editor at *Beyond* wants stories "with good characterization, conflict, and a resolution, not necessarily a happy ending, that holds out some hope of a meaningful future for the human race."

FOR ADDITIONAL READING

How to Write Tales of Horror, Fantasy, & Science Fiction, by J. N. Williamson. (Writer's Digest Books)

Plotting and Writing Science Fiction, by Patricia Highsmith. (The Writer)

THE MYSTERY AND DETECTIVE MARKET

Crime, it's been said, is big business. No one would argue that it's flourishing. And people's interest in the mystery and detective story is as keen, if not keener, than ever. Mystery and detective magazines continue to be excellent markets for the freelancer. All publications in the field depend heavily on freelance material and most pay average rates ($250 to $500) on acceptance.

THE CONTEMPORARY MYSTERY STORY

Many still think of the mystery as the old Sherlock Holmes whodunit but the genre now includes everything from the whodunit to the spy story, the thriller and the caper. Like everything else, the mystery has suffered (or enjoyed, depending on your view) changes in the last three decades. Says Bruce Cassiday, former editor of *Argosy* and prolific mystery fictioneer, "Like it or not, the Second World War changed the mystery story from a tale of death to a tale of megadeath, from a tale of deductive simplicity to a tale of scientific complexity, and from a tale of simple treasure or stolen loot to a tale of missing atomic formulas or lost psyches. Likewise, it shifted the mystery story from the drawing rooms of the solid middle (or upper) class to the streets and alleys of a troubled populace in social, racial, political, and economic ferment."

As the name of the genre implies, there has to be a mystery of some type involved, an unknown riddle or puzzle to solve, but nowadays the problem can be set against a broad range of both physical and psychological turmoil never used or conceived of in the past. At the same time, as John D. MacDonald tells us, today's impatient readers want "more suspense than mystification, more action than cerebration. Purists will not recognize the novel of action and suspense as a mystery. Indeed, they will be content with flatness of character, so long as there is a carefully interwoven web of clue and counter-clue. Unfortunately the purists do not form a sufficiently large market." MacDonald goes on to say, "There is nothing more dreadful than the 'mystery' novel of action and suspense wherein the characters have that peculiar woodenness characteristic of the English school of the mystery story, genus 1925....as the mystery story [of today] becomes less dependent on intricacy of plot and detection, it becomes ever more dependent on the depicting of characters 'in the round.' And as the characters in mystery fiction become ever more fully realized, the dividing line between the mystery and the straight novel becomes constantly more vague...."

A word about the mystery novel market: this is a field for which the reading public's appetite is never sated. While mainstream novels are often a hit-and-miss proposition for a publisher, it can reasonably be assured that a mystery novel will at least sell enough copies to break even. People love mysteries and many prefer to read the same story over and over again with only minor or superficial changes in plot, setting, characters and title. In spite of what was said above about the growing sophistication of the mystery story, this type of formula mystery still thrives.

The Detective, True-Crime Or Sensational Story

While the mystery genre has undergone sophistication and change, the true-crime or detective story still depends less on the people involved than on the crime and its solution. Here is the basic story virtually stripped to the bone: "Purpose versus obstacle in conflict." The purpose is to discover who perpetrated a certain crime (or a rash of crimes), the obstacle is the suspect's attempts to evade capture and the conflict is the work of the police in trying to find him.

The magazines devoted to the true-crime story buy somewhere in the neighborhood of at least 350 stories a month from freelancers. Other magazines of all types buy about 50 monthly. Men's magazines, general magazines, some city magazines and an increasing number of airline magazines buy this type of material.

Some tips on writing for this particular market: be adept and good at research (this applies to mystery and detective fiction as well as to true-crime); be on good terms with the police in the area in which your story occurred; hang around the local police station until you've blended into the woodwork; own and know how to use a camera (the magazines that buy true-crime stories want pictures); read the newspapers (the crimes must be current); put a lot of local color into your stories, thus creating an on-the-spot tone; know how to avoid lawsuits (employ the term "alleged" and its synonyms as though your life depended on it); and *always* know the magazine you are trying to write for and send a query first.

What The Editors Say

As in other markets, editors in the mystery and detective field complain of dull, pedestrian writing, unbelievable plots, stories lacking emotional appeal, trite, overworked ideas, non- professional writing and stories that do not meet *their* requirements. An editor at a leading mystery magazine recommended that potential contributors "read the magazine for its policy. Start with short (never novelettes) material first, put it aside and later revise objectively what you've written." From another editor: "We want the best mystery stories of our time. We do not want fact-detective cases or true stories; this is a fiction magazine."

In the case of the true detective market, editors at the DETECTIVE FILES GROUP advise freelancers to be neat, clear and prompt and read previous issues of the magazines in this group. From the OFFICIAL DETECTIVE GROUP: "Read the magazines for style, approach, legal savvy.

Most freelance submissions lack understanding of our legal requirements and problems. We are actively trying to develop new writers. Ideally, we like to work with a reporter for a daily in a city where he may be on a police or court beat. We find we can more easily train this type of writer, and educate him in the legal pitfalls of our specialized material, than is possible or practical with a writer without news experience. We use 30 stories a month, minimum, which is a lot of material. We have, upon occasion, given assignments to a reporter who calls or writes in with a query. We have developed dozens of good magazine writers, many of whom went on to write good books."

FOR ADDITIONAL READING

Writing Mystery and Crime Fiction, edited by Sylvia K. Burack. (The Writer)

Writing the Modern Mystery, by Barbara Norville. (Writer's Digest Books)

MEN'S MAGAZINES

For the past three decades, there has been an ever-widening gap between the outdoor, adventure/mystery, action magazines slanted toward the male audience, and the so-called 'adult' magazines which are sex-oriented, although some of the more successful (*Playboy* being a prime example) are publishing top-quality fiction and nonfiction—and are among the top-paying magazine markets, as well as the most competitive.

If you are planning to write for the 'adult' magazines it is vital that you study recent issues. At one end of the scale you'll find such magazines as *Chic, Fling* and *Uncensored Letters*, which require heavily sex-oriented material and rather simple writing style, to *Playboy* and *Penthouse* that use sophisticated, quality fiction and well-researched articles that are timely and written with wit and insight. The more erotic the magazine the less payment the author receives.

At the top of the pay scale is *Playboy*, paying a minimum of $3000 for a 3,000-5,000 word article, and $2000 for fiction. *Penthouse* rates are slightly lower, but still very high. Unless you have some excellent credits or a most unusual subject, it is best to submit to some of the lesser markets where the competition is not as fierce.

You will discover that there are several hundred erotic magazines on display in the larger adult bookstores, many of which go out of business after publishing one or two issues. Although few of these fly-by-nighters use freelance material, the majority pay very little, and often disappear before paying any of their authors.

Aside from the adult men's magazines there are many other categories which, although appealing primarily to the male audience, are being read more and more by women as well. In the past decade little growth has been seen in the number of detective/mystery magazines, western and action magazines. Unfortunately the rates of payment have also been stagnant. The primary changes in these markets have been in the editorial concept. Stories must be far more realistic and sophisticated, the characters must be more fully developed and the plotline plausible and believable.

The number of science fiction and fantasy magazines has increased substantially, but here also the editors insist on strong, realistic science fiction with human-centered stories. As one editor says, the stories must be strong and realistic, with believable people doing believable things—regardless of how fantastic the background might be.

Specialized Male-Oriented Markets

With the demise over the last twenty years of many of the all-purpose magazines, we have entered the era of the specialized publication, both in male-oriented and female-oriented periodicals. In the field of boating there are now over twenty magazines (not counting some 15 magazines devoted to other water sports); more than forty hunting and fishing magazines (there was a time when *Outdoor Life, Field and Stream,* and *Sports Afield* monopolized this market).

Today there are magazines that specialize in Kung-Fu, and Karate, in marathon running, weight lifting, racquetball, hang gliding, pigeon racing and skydiving, and many more.

Although many of these specialty magazines have relatively small circulations and their rates of payment are likewise small, ranging from $25.00 for an article to $500 if accepted by one of the more popular publications (like *The Runner* or *Golf Magazine*), they do offter some excellent opportunities for the beginning writer, especially one who has a particular interest or expertise in one of these specialized fields.

Another expanding market is in the field of travel and camping. Not only are there numerous travel-oriented magazines, such as the various in-flight publications, plus those sponsored by automobile clubs and automobile manufacturers, but with the continued growth of the camper and camper-trailer, more and more magazines dealing with 'the great outdoors' are coming on the scene. At last count more than 50 publications were reaching this audience.

Military-oriented magazines are also on the increase, with most using a considerable amount of freelance material. Some of these include *Soldier of Fortune, Military Lifestyle, Vietnam Magazine, Overseas!, Infantry,* and *Military Review.*

WOMEN'S MAGAZINES

The time has long passed when we could speak of "the women's magazine market" as if it were a single, monolithic entity, one creature made up of essentially similar parts. Like the rest of the magazine industry, the women's market has discovered "differentiation". And therein lies the strength of the market for today's freelancer.

"Differentiation" is a business management concept. It means that businesses are defining specific target populations and providing products to fill the unique needs of those market niches. While old standbys of the women's market, like *Good Housekeeping* or *Ladies Home Journal*, buy less unsolicited material, new "niche" markets spring up almost daily. Designed to meet specialized needs of sharply limited segments of the populace, such magazines welcome freelance submissions, if they are carefully targeted and researched for specific audiences. Today we see magazines designed for women in the martial arts, women who live in the country, women who practice charismatic Christianity, women executives, college students, bowlers and engineers.

At the same time the old standbys are themselves differentiating more than ever. Though you'll find both *Woman's World* and *Family Circle* at the supermarket checkout stand, the readership of the two magazines is strikingly different. Women who buy *Mademoiselle* for the fiction are not likely to be reading *True Romances* on the side.

Some of the women's magazines are as bold in their approach to the modern lifestyle as the best-known 'adult' men's magazines. *Playgirl* has its male centerfolds and articles and stories that serve the wants of contemporary women. *Ms.* treats women's changing lifestyles in a different fashion, as does *New Woman*.

Self-awareness and development—physical, mental, and psychic—are popular themes with many magazines, including some of those already mentioned, but it is a central theme of magazines such as *New Body*, *Self*, *Going Slim*, and *Soma*.

The 'shelter' magazines —usually considered a part of the women's market—have also undergone substantial changes in the past several years. These range from the practical, modest-budget magazines such as *Home* and the urban-oriented *Metropolitan Home* to the highly sophisticated, affluency-oriented *Architectural Digest*. In the middle range are *House and Garden*, *Better Homes and Gardens*, and *Good Housekeeping*, which cover not only home subjects but also topics of widespread interest to women or general audiences.

Personal experience articles are popular with many of the women's magazines, and some have specific departments for these subjects. *Mothers Today*, *Redbook*, *Woman*, *Good Housekeeping*, and *Farm Wife News* are among those seeking such material. Payment of $750 is offered by some of the better markets for personal experience pieces. At the other end of the scale are plentiful markets for short material—such as tips, brief anecdotes, cooking hints, etc.—which can be written quickly and may produce a steady flow of checks, however small they might be ($15 to $50 would be the range).

How-to articles are also popular with women's magazines, whether the subject is organizing a community political campaign, maintaining your car, or creating an arts-and-craft project. Payments offered for such articles range from $50 for the smaller magazines to $500 or more for the major, mass-circulation markets.

As the market differentiates, so do rates and methods of payment. Many magazines in this market still pay on acceptance, but the smaller and newer ones may not.

Freshness of idea and execution, thorough research and tight focus are likewise more important than ever today, as magazines specialize to serve knowledgeable audiences.

The trend toward "niche publishing" makes it imperative to study individual markets before submitting to them. Hit-and-miss submissions discredit freelancers in general and close down accessibility to markets for everyone.

THE CONFESSION MARKET

Numerous changes have occurred in the women's confession magazine field. Editorially many of the confessions have become educational as well as entertaining. The 'story-article' based on extensive research has replaced the out-and-out tear jerker. More recently, the confession magazines were in deep financial trouble, due to higher costs of paper, printing, staff. The result has been changes in ownership, more combining into 'confession groups,' and suspension of publication of many of the magazines.

In the past decade, the number of confession magazines has decreased from 20 to a dozen, and most of these are published by two different publishers.

Readership, however, remains steady, and it is estimated that over 5,000,000 women are reading confession magazines each month.

The rates, on the other hand, have increased in some cases. Lexington Library, whose publications are aimed mostly at the black and ethnic reader, has upped its pay from one cent a word to 8-20 cents a word. However, the Macfadden Women's Group has not raised its rate of pay, still offering 3 to 5 cents a word, with payment on publication or later.

Confessions remain as one of the best potential markets for freelancers. Several of the confession magazines depend 100% on unsolicited freelance material. The Macfadden group uses over 90% unsolicited, with the balance from regular contributors. About 90% of the material used in Sterling Library magazines is unsolicited.

Comments Made By Confession Magazine Editors

The reasons given most by confession magazine editors for rejection are 1) trite, overworked ideas, 2) not believable, 3) lack of emotional appeal, 4) non-professional, 5) dull pedestrian writing. All of the editors responding indicated that the freelance material was of considerable value, in spite of the shortcomings.

True Romance editors say, "This field is wide open to freelancers. It can be a great market for beginners to break into, but so often they fail to read the magazine they're submitting to . . . We keep up with the trends and so should those writing for us."

The editor of *Black Romance* says, "Major problems are that the plot isn't thick enough, characters are undefined, the dialogue is flimsy or thin, and there is no conflict or tension...Romance stories seem more real if they are based upon timely events and depict romance as it is now...The AIDS and crack epidemics have an impact on romance. Not keeping up with the times make for superficial stories."

True Confessions editors say, "Writers should keep in mind that our readers are young, high school educated, blue-collar wives and mothers. Stories intended for us should be timely, exciting, and emotional, and they should be centered around the problems that face today's young women. Every story should have a strong romantic interest, and every plot should reach an exciting climax. All stories should be narrated in the first person and have a strong moral tone."

Another suggestion was that the author should "make the story *something that could happen to you.*"

"We are in need of stories dealing with current sexual issues: homosexuality, abortion, incest, etc.," notes the editor of *Real Confessions* and *Modern Love*. "Do not over-plot. Often there are too many ideas for one story."

How To Write For The Confessions

While there are special techniques used in the confession story, it is fundamentally little different from any other short story. The confession story has, generally, plot, climax, suspense, characterization, etc.. However, there are certain guidelines and writing techniques required to effectively write this type of story:

1. Always write in the first person.
2. Make your narrator likable, but make the problem she faces a staggering one.
3. Keep the story believable.
4. Make the reader sympathetic toward the narrator.
5. Employ emotional conflicts of ordinary people.

6. Write the story in scenes and keep the writing tight.
7. Approach each story you write with a fresh angle.
8. Inspire the reader to have hope.

THE INSPIRATIONAL MARKET

The religious and inspirational markets are multi-faceted, ranging from slick paper magazines to tabloids and from local church news to comments on world affairs.

Some demand conformity to their own doctrines while others welcome controversy on a variety of subjects. Perhaps more than in any other field, it is vital to obtain and study copies of the publications thoroughly to see if your material is appropriate. Be aware of the taboos which many of these magazines observe. For example, don't be casual or flippant about tobacco or liquor in articles submitted to Seventh Day Adventist or Mennonite magazines. However, many of these publications have become much more sophisticated in their approach to religion and accept material that may be critical, providing it is constructive.

Religious and inspirational magazines buy a great deal of freelance material and are excellent starting places for new writers. A sale is always more uplifting than continued rejection even if the pay may be low. There are also many writers who, after learning how to slant their material to particular markets, make a comfortable living writing for the religious market.

The religious market is one of the few remaining outlets for short fiction and poetry. Many religious magazines are slanted toward children and young adults, presenting an excellent opportunity for those who wish to break into the juvenile field. There is an increasing demand for photos with articles. Such important details a writer learns as he or she studies the market intensively.

Religious Magazine Survey Results

In response to a recent survey, several editors reported receiving from 1,000 to less than 500 manuscripts per year. Few seemed heavily loaded with a backlog of material. The highest number of "over the transom" submissions was somewhat in excess of 5,000, a goodly number, but not bad when compared with the 50,000 manuscripts a year received by some of the larger magazines.

This does not imply an easy market. A writer should seriously study the slant of a particular publication before investing in postage. Some of the major complaints from editors:

- "Writers need to read the magazine and submit relevant material."
- "Articles not targeted to our readers."
- "Not original."
- "Nothing fresh to say."
- "Poorly written."

One magazine editor suggested the following as elements of a "good" article: 1) It must prove something; 2) It must have impact, must make a difference; 3) Should have suspense and conflict; 4) Should be people-oriented; 5) Striking lead; 6) Satisfying ending; 7) Well researched; 8) Well constructed; 9) Lively anecdotes; 10) Involve a reader's mind, emotions, heart, senses.

One Baptist editor says, "You almost need to be a born again Christian to write for us." Some Baptist editors do not feel this way.

There is a high degree of interest in interviews with outstanding members of local churches, church people on the world or national level, and with prominent laymen who have important ideas about religion. Nearly always, the interest in these interviews is enhanced if the subject is a member of the magazine's denomination.

The religious market is also interested in current social or political problems, how their members are affected and how to help their readers cope with adversity.

Many beginning writers shun religious markets, "because I'm not religious." Careful study shows that much material in religious magazines is not blatantly religious. It is, however, always moral, an important distinction to keep in mind.

The inspirational article has great potential both in the religious and secular markets, but many writers have trouble understanding its structure. One writer who sold many articles of this type said she simply analyzed, in detail, the structure of a very moving piece published in one magazine, and outlined her idea in the same manner. She has sold that same article numerous times. "Whenever I read an article I like, I continue to look for the skeleton," she reports. "Then I try to figure out construction specifics." She applies the method in many types of writing. Be sure, however, that you copy only the pattern, not the words, of your "teacher."

Humorous articles for these markets are acceptable but one should avoid satirical or ethnic humor.

Pay ranges from free copies to several hundred dollars. Method of payment is either on acceptance or on publication, the former being the most desirable for the writer, of course.

Low payment rates may not be as much as a handicap as one might think at first. Many religious markets accept multiple submissions and also buy second rights. It is important to check new directories carefully, since magazines are especially likely to change policies when a new editor takes charge. Keep market directories as current as possible.

Before submitting a manuscript—even before writing it—a writer should ask for guidelines and a sample copy. Many will send free copies, others charge, but it's a good investment.

Don't forget

1. Write in a popular understandable style, assuming a general readership. Avoid cheap sentimentality.

2. Revise and rewrite—hone and polish as if it were a sculpture to be displayed.
3. Do the best work possible. Don't expect an editor to correct spelling, punctuation, or find the exact word to convey intended meaning. Be sure the manuscript says what it is meant to say.
4. Use reference materials: dictionary, Bible, thesaurus, grammar handbook, sources—and refer to them often. Cite all quotations and paraphrases taken from other sources. Be familiar with the type of material individual publishers want.
5. Don't expect second-rate material to be accepted just because it is "religious."

Religious Book Publishers

Denominational presses print hundreds of books each year. Partly because of the financial crunch felt by lay publishers, their percentage of the total book market is increasing.

Sales of books from religious publishing houses and the religious publishing divisions of general publishing houses have risen dramatically, and most experts believe the trend will continue. A number of Christian books have achieved million-plus in-print levels, and some are well above 2 million. Many others are in the high six-figure bracket. A few, such as *The Cross and the Switchblade* (15 million sold) are multi-million sellers.

Major publishers of secular books are strengthening or promoting their religious books divisions. These include Prentice-Hall, Harper & Row, Ballantine, Atheneum, Macmillan and Simon & Schuster. Religious publishing houses, on the other hand, are branching into categories, such as romances, formerly thought the exclusive province of secular publishers.

The marketing organization for religious books has grown even more dramatically. The number of Christian bookstores has grown six-fold in the past 25 years, and their location and size have become increasingly prominent.

As in selling to magazines, it is imperative that one study the market. Know certain houses' specialities. Religious magazines carry advertisements for recently released books, so one can become familiar with book markets and study a magazine at the same time. A thorough study of market directories is again in order. It's a golden opportunity that is often overlooked.

FOR ADDITIONAL READING

Writing to Inspire: A Guide to Writing and Publishing for the Expanding Religous Market, by William Gentz, Lee Roddy, and others. (Writer's Digest Books)
The Christian Writer's Handbook, by Margaret J. Anderson. (Harper & Row)
Writing Religiously: A Guide to Writing Nonfiction Religious Books, by Don M. Aycock and Leonard George Goss. (Mott Media)
Inspirational Writers' Market Guide, by Sally E. Stuart. (Joy Publishing)

THE EDUCATIONAL THEATRE

For those who have ambitions to be playwrights, the most logical place to start is with the educational theatre. Although standards of quality have risen in amateur productions, the competition is far less and there is an increasing demand by high school and college drama programs.

Unlike major-length writing for the Broadway or professional stage, in which publication is one of several secondary effects, publication becomes almost an end in itself for writers of short stage pieces. Only through this medium can they hope to carry their message to the actors of the educational stage.

No play should be published, however, nor any move made toward publication until the script has seen at least one production. The coordinator of a nearby college lab theatre or the director of a respected high school program will frequently be open to new scripts. Contact such people. Production in one of these arenas is crucial. Unlike pure print media, the playscript finds its true culmination onstage. Only when the play is mounted will the playwright be able to judge accurately if his sufferings have borne fruit.

But first, the vehicle itself.

One word should stay in the playwright's mind from the typing of "At rise,"—validity. Today's young actors have seen live coverage of the murders of John Kennedy and Lee Harvey Oswald and witnessed the exposure of national figures as frauds. Such performers have no interest in adolescent themes. Unless the subject is important, the script is valueless.

Practical Considerations

The production budgets of the theatre schools remain meager. This can be turned to the playwright's advantage if he will think in terms of "theatricality." Where the realistic producer insists on forest backdrops and three-dimensional trees, his theatrical counterpart opts for a single stylized tree. Through such simplicity we gain an advantage over the electronic and film media in that we reap a greater personal involvement with our audience, the magic Coleridge called, "...the willing suspension of disbelief."

While it is usually best to limit settings in a one-act to a single location, theatricality makes multi-settings possible. In certain plays, sets as such may be eliminated altogether. Jerome McDonough's *Asylum* uses only one hand prop, a wheelchair. The actors define their own areas and mime all other props. This is an extreme example, but the spirit suggests the possibilities.

Period plays, those which are fixed in time, are risky. Costuming a period piece accurately is expensive. The playwright may avoid this problem by either writing in the contemporary vein or by releasing his script from time, consciously striving for universality. Beckett's *Waiting for Godot* and Wilder's *Our Town* are always in the present, at least in meaning. The central theme of *Filiation*, one of McDonough's early works, is an overhanging fear of the police state. It could take place in Nazi Germany or some nameless future society.

School producers normally have an uneven balance of the sexes. There are more girls than boys. Women are in their ascendency, so why not celebrate this on our stage? Baker's Plays has questioned the need to designate a certain character in *Dirge* as male and the change was as simple as altering the character's name and doing a minor re-write. In extremely modern, theatrical plays the gender of the actor may even be unimportant. *Fables* is performed by ten actors, only two of whom must be male or female.

Most publishers and producers tend to avoid the very small cast show (four or less) but conversely, mob scenes find few productions. Seven to twelve characters is average but this is only a guideline. If a vehicle needs three people, as *The Betrothed*, four is too many. Never compromise a script artistically.

In episodic or vignetted plays (and some standard plays), a troupe of ten, say, may play many roles through double- or triple-casting. *Asylum* has over thirty named characters, but its five scenes may be mounted by a cast of twelve. (In the episodic work, several short scenes enlarge upon a central theme.)

Publishers are overwhelmed with submissions. Samuel French, for example, receives over 2,000 scripts a year. I.E. Clark refuses to have his company listed in the national writer's magazines because he cannot handle such a volume. All this is to warn that play publishers are slow in reporting on scripts. Rather than the typical sixty-day period before the follow-up discreet inquiry goes to the editor, the playwright should wait three to four months. Suspense periods of six to eight months are not, sadly, uncommon.

Submit only the original typing, not a photo copy, unless you are already known to the editor. Some editors state that multiple submissions are all right in play publishing but this is a frightening practice. What if two companies want the same piece? There are too few editors in this field to make any enemies. On the positive side, play editors are some of the warmest people in all publishing.

Format

Double-space throughout when submitting to a publisher. (Producer's requirements differ somewhat.) Paper-clip the pages together and include the author's name and that of the play on each page.

Capitalize the character's name, follow it with a colon and write the dialogue line. Short stage directions within the text are placed in parentheses. Use a wide left-hand margin. This format differs from that in other texts but no editor has ever complained.

Which House?

The number of play publishers is painfully small. As in all writing, the penman must know the market. The play firms will forward their catalogs for the price of postage and the playwright should study all catalogs and a few representative scripts of each company.

If a play is placed with one of the larger companies, it will find itself among the giants of the theatre and reach the widest possible audience. The big catalogs may, however, submerge a work beneath the mass of titles. A small firm has a narrower audience but individual scripts stand out. On balance, an equal number of productions will probably result from either house. The author must finally judge the company. Quality, not size or locations, should be his watchword.

Payday

Most companies offer royalties ranging from twenty-five to fifty percent of performance revenues with short plays generally demanding a fee of ten to fifteen dollars per performance. Some companies also offer a book royalty spanning a nickel per copy to ten percent of retail price.

A less common practice is the outright purchase of the rights to a play. A piece which was dashed off in a few hours is easier to release in this way than one over which much blood has been spilled. Hopefully, outright purchase of scripts will go the way of the Edsel.

Curtain Call

Write, re-write, read, produce, re-write and publish. It's strange how seeing a familiar name of the front of a tiny book makes all that worthwhile.

WRITING FOR THE YOUTH THEATRE

(Adapted from a report by Henry Musmanno)

The phrase, youth theater, is used to describe theater for children, teenagers, and young adults. A prerequisite is an understanding of young people, as well as a working knowledge of the stage. If you are not familiar with writing for the theater, you should affiliate with a small, local theater group and study books on play construction.

Before submitting to a *publisher*, your play should have had at least one production. *Producers*, on the other hand, prefer that your play has not been produced.

The Proper Format

1. Title page, with name and address in upper left hand corner.
2. Last name and brief title of the play at the top of each page.
3. Cast of characters, with a brief description of main characters.
4. Detailed description of each set.
5. Time and place of central action.
6. Dialogue: Name of character speaking, centered and in capital letters, above his or her speech.
7. Stage directions in parentheses, not in caps. For longer, detailed stage directions, indent, block, and place in parentheses. Directions should be in present tense.
8. Double space.
9. Computer print acceptable if letter quality.
10. Include SASE.
11. If your play is a musical or has music in it, enclose a cassette of the music.
12. Playing time: One act, 30 to 40 minutes. Full length, two hours. Ninety-minute dramas are sometimes accepted.
13. Mail in a two or three-ring binder.

Some Practical Aspects

Since producers work on a meager budget and with limited facilities, keep the following in mind:
1. Cast should be small. Between four and 12 characters are preferable. Less than four require too much of a load for amateurs.
2. If possible, use more female characters than male. Usually more females are available for amateur productions.
3. Limit the action to one set, or a unit set.
4. Avoid the use of period pieces requiring expensive sets or costumes.
5. Elaborate props should be avoided, for obvious reasons.

Some Important Suggestions

1. Start the action early.
2. Keep exposition to a minimum. Audiences prefer action to long explanations of things that happened in the past.
3. Use crisp, original dialogue that reveals character.
4. Conflict is essential.
5. Develop plot through your characters.
6. Character motivation must be believable.
7. Have a strong protagonist and antagonist.
8. Build to a strong, logical climax.
9. Keep in mind the audience you are writing for.
10. Keep your stage directions to a minimum.

Pertinent Information

Publishers usually purchase all rights. Most producers buy negotiable rights or production rights in which the rights revert back to the playwright when the production closes.

Since it takes a long time for publishers and producers to respond, simultaneous submissions are permissible.

The number of plays published each year varies with each company. The range is from four to 35. The largest publisher is Contemporary Drama Service. Production companies produce from three to ten plays a year, with an average of seven.

Pay Scales

PUBLISHERS: Most pay 25 to 50 percent royalties each time your play is produced, and a ten percent book royalty for each copy of your play that is sold.

PRODUCERS: These companies have a great variance in pay scales. Some buy your manuscript outright, others pay per performance.

FILLERS AND SHORT ARTICLES

Fillers and short articles are generally brief nonfiction pieces. They may consist of a single paragraph (a filler) or a maximum of 1,000 words. Since magazines have strict word limits on short pieces, be sure to tailor your material to the magazine's exact requirements.

Facts About the Short Article Market

Many persons are under the mistaken impression that a filler is easy to write, and for that reason a steady stream of this material reaches the editor's desk. Too many writers are constantly turning out completely unsuitable material. In this field, as in others, editors demand and expect professional quality. Only when one has exceptional material (and this is rare) is an amateurish presentation accepted.

Avoid the obvious. Any editorial office could assign a stenographer to read an encyclopedia and prepare a short piece on any of hundreds of subects. Any clerk could rewrite a newspaper item, simply condensing what had been printed in the press. It should be obvious that if a writer does either of these, s/he is consigning his article to rejection in advance. The factual article based on research may be salable only if the research covers a number of sources and comprises thereby a job editors are willing to pay someone else to do. A newspaper rewrite may prove salable only if the writer follows it up to develop an original slant he or she has discovered or if the writer can add materially to what has been published.

There may be an exception to the foregoing. If one is very clever with words and can state facts, even those that derive from one source alone, in a highly entertaining or amusing way, he or she may may then find a market for a short item. As this is a job for a skilled writer, it is best for most persons who want to write short articles to avoid rewriting a single piece.

Editorial Practices

A few magazines will not return very brief (under 100 words) fillers, even if return postage is sent. If you know that the magazine will not return material, it is well to state on your manuscript that it will be offered to other sources if not accepted within sixty days. Rates of payment vary greatly.

Some magazines that regularly pay on acceptance will pay for brief material on publication. Rates usually are higher for very short material, but nevertheless, they range from one to five cents a word or much more, depending upon the market. Some magazines require a statement of the source of your information; if you do not include this on your manuscript, be prepared to give it.

Preparation of Manuscripts

Even though your piece may be short, it is well to type it on a full 8-1/2 x 11 sheet. One writer separated the paper into three equal parts by having it perforated. This makes for easy separation of fillers. If such device is not employed, it is best to type each one on a full-sized sheet.

Competition for acceptances is keen. While there is a wide market, much of it is highly specialized; one is unlikely to earn a living in this area or make much money, but occasional sales are entirely possible, valued for their encouragement as well as for whatever payment they may bring.

Editors are unlikely to have confidence in or to pay much attention to poorly prepared manuscripts. It is a waste of time and postage to send out anything less attractively prepared than you are able to make it.

You must be absolutely sure of your facts when writing about factual subjects. Print this adage on a card, and keep it before you:

I WILL REVISE CAREFULLY TO ELIMINATE ERRORS IN SPELLING AND PUNCTUATION. I WILL TYPE MY MANUSCRIPT ATTRACTIVELY. A SELF- ADDRESSED STAMPED ENVELOPE WILL BE SENT WITH EACH SUBMISSION. I WILL KEEP ACCURATE RECORDS. WHEN NECESSARY, I WILL TELL THE EDITOR WHAT MY SOURCES OF INFORMATION ARE:

How to Write Fillers and Short Articles

A filler or short article should range from 30 to 40 words to a maximum of 1,000 words. How you write is less important than what you have to say and the freshness and appropriateness of your piece. Only when writing a short essay may style be important, and then it must be of exceptional merit to be salable. When writing about historical facts, try to tie up your subject with something current. Contrast, parallel or underscore your material with something that ties in with something of significance *today*. Brevity is the rule with all fillers and short articles.

What Editors Want

The following outline covers virtually every type of adult filler or short article for which there is any market at all:

1.   QUOTATIONS
    (a)   Wise or witty sayings
    (b)   Material for special departments
    (c)   Epigrams
    (d)   Amusing news breaks
    (e)   Little known facts

2. EDITORIALS
   (a) Guest editorials
   (b) Inspirational
   (c) Opinions (on politics, religion, etc.)

3. GAMES
   (a) Guest editorials
   (b) Tests
   (c) Puzzles

4. FACTUAL
   (a) The odd or unusual
   (b) Helpful knowledge
   (c) Historical
   (d) Personal
   (e) News
   (f) Newspaper or magazine clippings (limited market)

5. TRUE ACCOUNTS
   (a) Adventures
   (b) ESP or other supernatural experience
   (c) Personal experience as an example to others

6. ANECDOTES
   (a) Interesting accounts of the famous
   (b) Short humor
   (c) Jokes
   (d) Humorous or satirical comments

7. FEATURES
   (a) Travel
   (b) Personalities
   (c) Industries, occupations, public endeavors briefly reported

8. HOW-TO
   (a) How to make useful or decorative things
   (b) How to do things easier or more economically
   (c) How to save money
   (d) Self-help
   (e) Recipes

9.   CHILDREN: Following is a list of current filler and short article requirements as stated by editors of juvenile magazines:

Puzzles and quizzes
Crossword puzzles
Party and other games
Handcrafts
Party ideas
Puzzles on Bible subjects
One act plays
Jokes and short humor
Simple songs
Interesting bits of information

Where to Send Your Material

A great variety of publications use fillers and short articles. The list is too changeable to warrant listing here. To do so would be to defeat one of the main elements of successful marketing: aggressiveness. It should be sufficient to point out these generalities about markets; almost any magazine will use an occasional short piece if it is interesting and unusual enough and is in line with its editorial policy.

Tip: Whenever you read or scan a magazine, see if short articles are used. Overlook no opportunity to check publications and to note the type of material or approach used. An alert and energetic person specializing in writing short articles and fillers can find them to be reasonably rewarding.

WHAT SYNDICATION IS ALL ABOUT

There are many misconceptions about syndicates and syndications. Many freelancers relate syndicates to Charles Schultz and his creation, "Peanuts," or Jack Anderson or Art Buchwald, who have turned syndication into a million dollar business. Granted that lucrative opportunities exist, it is a difficult and low-paying field for unestablished freelancers.

A syndicate is, in effect, a kind of agent, marketing the writer's material for a fee. Syndicates differ from agents in some respects: A literary agency generally handles books while a syndicate more often handles shorter material, such as a column, a comic strip, cartoons, crossword puzzles, filler items, etc. A literary agency usually charges a 10 percent commission, but a syndicate usually splits with the author on a 50/50 basis, 40/60, or sometimes 30/70, the lower percentage going to the author. Another difference is that a syndicate usually has established outlets (most often, newspapers) for the material it is selling, whereas an agent must seek out the right publisher for the right book.

Most of the successful syndicated authors work with established syndicates under contract. However, it is possible to operate independently as a self-syndicated freelancer. The obvious advantage is that you retain all of the profits. On the negative side, you also pay all of the expenses of producing and selling your material. In most cases, self-syndication is necessary, since established syndicates are hesitant about contracting with unknown or little known writers.

A complete list of syndicates, including the names of various columns and features they handle, can be found in *Editor and Publisher Syndicate Directory*.

Facts You Should Know About Self-Syndications

Your first decision, if considering self-syndication, is to select a subject area and determine whether you have a new idea, a new approach, the knowledge or the research facilities for a continuing column or feature. Some of the more common topics are family, finance, self-improvement, hobbies, inspiration, sports, music, etc.

Unless you feel strongly about syndicating the material yourself, you should attempt initially to contact established syndicates to determine if any will accept it and sell it for you. This is a faster road to success and usually with greater financial rewards, even with the split of the income.

If you have no success with a syndicate, and are convinced that you have developed material of interest to a mass audience (*this is a must*), your next step is to decide whether you are going to write a daily column, a twice or three times a week column, or a weekly column. You must also decide on the length of the column, and each should be the same. It will have a better chance if it is short, not more than 500 words. You will have to work up at least six columns if you plan to submit it to weekly papers, and preferably a dozen if you are submitting to daily papers.

Once you have completed your columns, you can type them on a 20-lb bond paper, double-spaced, and make machine copies to send to the various newspapers. Or if your budget will allow, you can actually have the columns set in type and as many proofs pulled as you need. This is somewhat more professional, but if you use this method, be sure to have them set to the standard column width of the average newspaper.

You have now completed the easy part. You will need a list of newspapers (at least 100) to which you can submit your material. The *Editor and Publisher Year Book* lists all of the daily and weekly newspapers in the United States, as well as the name of the editors and other pertinent information. Include a cover letter giving a brief rundown on the nature of the column and why you think it is of value, as well as any credentials you might have for writing it. Be sure to include the cost of the column. If you plan a daily column, you might ask $5.00 a week (for either 5 or 6 columns). If a weekly, about $3.00 per week is average. Do as much selling as you can, without insulting the intelligence of the editor.

It is possible (and discouraging) that you will receive no favorable response. In this case, you might contact some of the editors of local papers personally and offer them the column free of charge for a few weeks. Once you have a half dozen papers (perhaps all in your own state) running the column, you will have stronger credentials for attempting to sell it on a regional or national basis.

If you have a particular area of expertise, perhaps in some technical field, you may wish to consider a column for trade or business papers instead of newspapers. Your market is not as large, but the payment for an individual column may be greater. Once you have an established column, you will be able to approach the established syndicates and get a much warmer response.

Results Of A Survey Of The Syndicate Market

Of 50 syndicates surveyed, 21 responded. Seven stated that they welcome queries and proposals, accompanied by published writing samples, resumes showing the writer's credentials, or both. Eight will consider only completed material.

When asked about specific needs, there was a wide variety of responses, although a majority indicated "fresh, original ideas with wide appeal," were always in demand.

Only five provide requirement sheets, and all of these indicated requests must be accompanied by SASE (Self addressed stamped envelope). Several syndicates indicated that any material submitted without SASE would be destroyed without a reading.

Some syndicates split revenue with the author on a 50/50 basis on domestic sales, 80/20 on foreign sales. Many negotiate terms with the author. Others pay flat fees for one-shot or series material, ranging from $5 to $50 or more.

Syndicates seem to have no standards as far as rights purchased. Some purchase only the first publication rights, while six of those responding purchase all rights. A syndicate might purchase British rights only, another may request world rights, except for North America. Query for guidelines with SASE.

MARKET DIRECTORIES

Literary Market Place (LMP). Annually.

Comprehensive listing of book publishers, including American, Canadian, Micro-publishers. Provides names and titles of key personnel, when founded, number of titles published, and brief description of particular fields of interest. Also indicates if publisher is member of Association of American Publishers (AAP) and/or other significant associations.

Most complete listing of authors' agents available. Includes areas of interest and if agent is a member of the Society of Authors Representatives.

Excellent listing of editorial services, including specialities.

Electronic media listings, including names and addresses of TV networks, TV stations, radio and TV programs featuring books, and the key personnel at these stations.

Listings and information about writing courses, writer's conferences, prize contests, literary fellowships and grants.

Alphabetical listing of all companies and individuals appearing in LMP.

COMMENT: The best source for complete listing of book publishers and author's agents. Subject listing of publishers is most helpful. Although magazine listing is not comprehensive, classification of magazines by subject interest is useful.

Available from R. R. Bowker, 245 W. 17th St., New York, NY 10011.

International Literary Market Place. Annually.

Covers more than 9,000 publishers outside the United States and Canada. Also includes trade and professional organizations related to publishing abroad; also major bookstores, libraries, literary agencies, translators.

COMMENT: Companion volume to LMP, for those interested in foreign markets.

Available from R. R. Bowker, 245 W. 17th St., New York, NY 10011.

Writer's Market. Annually.

Most comprehensive general listing of popular markets for writers. Provides substantial information concerning editorial requirements, how to break in, rates and method of payment, names of editors, addresses and phone numbers.

Includes brief articles on writing and marketing practices of value to freelance writers.

COMMENT: One of the best reference sources for home use. Book publishing listing is not as complete as LMP, but provides more information on editorial needs.

Available from Writer's Digest, 1507 Dana Ave., Cincinnati, OH 45207.

Writer's Handbook. Annually.

Not as comprehensive a market guide as WM, but includes excellent listings of TV and play markets. Breakdown of magazine markets into 'fiction,' 'article,' and 'popular' is helpful.

Approximately 2/3 of the handbook is devoted to informative articles on many aspects of writing.

COMMENT: *Writer's Handbook* is mostly valued for its articles.

Available from The Writer, 120 Boylston St., Boston, MA 02116.

Standard Periodical Directory. Annually.

Over 62,000 listings of periodicals of all kinds (excluding newspapers) making it by far the largest listing of magazines published, with over 200 classifications.

COMMENT: Perhaps the best source for names and addresses of publishers for virtually every periodical published in the U.S. However, this directory provides minimal information on editorial requirements.

Available from Oxbridge Pub. Co., 150 Fifth Ave., New York, NY 10011.

Standard Rate and Data Service. Monthly.

SRDS publishes a variety of directories, designed primarily for advertising agencies and potential advertisers, but still useful for freelancers. SRDS directories of particular interest to writers are "Consumer Magazines and Farm Publications," "Business Publications," "Newspapers" and "Television."

Listings are classified by subjects and alphabetically. Except for a short "Editorial Profile," there is little information on editorial requirements.

COMMENT: The advantages of SRDS publications are their frequency and the demographic information on each publication's readership. The chief drawback is that these directories only list publications which accept advertising, although they are very comprehensive within those bounds.

Available from Standard Rate and Data Service, 5201 Old Orchard Rd., Skokie, IL 60076.

Ayer Directory of Newspapers and Periodicals. Annually.

Guide to publications printed in the United States and its territories, also Canada and Panama. Listing is alphabetical by state and city. Includes brief statistics about each locality. Lists frequency of publication, circulation, address, names of editor and publisher.

COMMENT: One of the most complete listings available of daily and weekly newspapers (including Sunday supplements), foreign language newspapers, trade publications and feature syndicates. Also lists general circulation magazines by areas of interest. No editorial requirements listed.

Available from N.W. Ayer & Son, West Washington Square, Philadelphia, PA 19106.

Editor and Publisher Year Book. Annually.

A basic listing of newspapers published in the United States and the leading newspapers throughout the world. Newspapers in the USA section are classified as daily, weekly, American Indian, Black, college, foreign language and special service.

Information of special value to freelancers includes syndicates and press services.

COMMENT: Perhaps the best source for names and addresses of U.S. newspapers; one of the most extensive listings available of foreign newspapers.

Available from Editor & Publisher Co., 575 Lexington Ave., New York, NY 10022.

International Writers' and Artists' Year Book. Annually.

This is one of the best books for writers that has ever been published on English language markets. Its major emphasis is on British and Irish markets, as well as journals and magazines in Australia, New Zealand and Africa. Theatre, film, radio and television markets are also listed; and numerous articles of importance to writers are included.

COMMENT: An excellent directory for those interested in writing for publications in the British Empire.

Available from Writer's Digest Books, 1507 Dana Ave., Cincinnati, OH 45207.

International Directory of Little Magazines and Small Presses. Annually.

This is an alphabetical directory of the smaller publishers generally omitted from WM and the LMP, with a paragraph on each press or publication, a subject index and a regional index arranged by zip code.

COMMENT: These markets offer the best opportunity for the beginning writer or for avant-garde or off-beat material. Since the mortality rate on these presses and publications is high, do not submit irreplaceable material.

Available from Dustbooks, PO Box 1056, Paradise, CA 95969.

Ulrich's International Periodicals Directory. Biennial.

Lists over 60,000 periodicals published throughout the world, classified by subject and indexed by titles. Includes publisher name and address, editor, and some information on editorial needs.

Ulrich's Quarterly. Quarterly.

A quarterly supplement to the biennial edition of the international directory which updates changes in any of the listings.

COMMENT: A very valuable set of tools for the writer proficient in foreign languages or with access to a good translator.

Available from R. R. Bowker, 245 W. 17th St., New York, NY 10011.

National Trade & Professional Associations of the U.S. & Canada. Annually.

Technically this is not a market directory, but is certainly the most comprehensive listing of associations being published today. Many of these associations publish newsletters or research reports or even magazines for their members. Almost all of them need qualified freelancers at one time or another. These associations are also good sources of information concerning trade magazines relevant to their members.

Listings are alphabetical with an extremely helpful "Key Word Index" in the back of the book, along with an "Executive Index." Includes list of labor unions also.

COMMENT: A storehouse of valuable information for the writer.

Available from Columbia Books, 1350 New York Ave., N.W. Suite 207, Washington, DC 20005.

The Religious Writer's Marketplace. Annually.

Most complete listing of North American publishers of religious materials. Over 1,500 listings.

Available from Running Press, 125 S. 22nd St., Philadelphia, PA 19103.

HOW TO WRITE A QUERY LETTER

While this chapter is devoted to marketing and how to sell what you write, one important ingredient, after you have selected your market, is to get the editor's attention. Writing a good query letter is the way.

Increasingly, editors are requesting that writers query them before sending a completed manuscript. The primary reason for this trend is to save staff time in the editorial department, since a judgement as to whether the subject matter would be of interest can be made quickly. This procedure also saves time and money for the author. Instead of waiting four or five months to obtain an answer concerning a manuscript, the author usually will get a response to a query within a few weeks.

Some writers feel that the only way a fair appraisal of their material can be made is for the editor to read it in its entirety. If a writer cannot write a convincing query letter, the chances are that his/her book or article lacks organization or a clear-cut theme. Once you realize that a query letter's main purpose is to convince the editor that your proposed material is something that is intriguing, important, and of interest to his readers, then you have the proper attitude toward writing the query.

Two preliminary steps are necessary before you draft your query:

1. Crystallize your idea so that you can present it in an interesting way.

2. Know your prospective market.

Know the policy of the magazine, and to what type of reader it is directed. A study of recent issues should provide the answers. In any event, read the guidelines if the editor provides them, or read the comments in the various market directories concerning editorial requirements.

Get yourself in the proper frame of mind. Take on the role of a sales person about to make a sales pitch to an editor. Now you are ready to write your letter.

Your opening statement should be calculated to arouse the editor's interest. It may be challenging, emotional, provocative, or practical. As one editor said at a writer's conference: "We want the author to seduce us with his or her idea."

You should quickly give the editor the substance of your article or book and why it should have appeal to his readers. Present your material through anecdotes or opinions. A brief quote from the work itself can help give the editor the flavor of the piece as well as an indication of how your writing sparkles. If it is an article query, present a few facts that it reveals, but briefly.

Offer some authority for the information contained in the article and also state why you are especially equipped to do this particular story. If other articles or books have been written on the subject, you should advise the editor why yours is different, either because of some exclusive material or because you have used a new approach.

Points to be included in your query:

The approximate number of words that will be in your finished manuscript.

How many photographs or other illustrations you will have (if any).

Advise that you will (or will not) do the article on speculation. Unless you have written for the publication previously, you should agree to do the article on speculation.

Limit your query to a maximum of two pages (one page is preferred).

Use standard size (8 1/2 x 11) letterhead and be sure that your name and address are included.

Single-space your letter.

Address the editor by name, if possible. In any case, send only an original letter (no machine copy).

Provide your credentials. Include education, writing credits, employment, only if they are pertinent to the material you plan to submit.

Always include SASE (self-addressed stamped envelope) with your query.

A query letter to a book publisher need not be much different from one written to a magazine editor. The same pre-preparation, the same calculated effort to arouse interest and 'sell' the editor are essential.

Don't ask the editor if you may send the manuscript. Say instead that you will be pleased to send completed chapters, a detailed outline, or the finished manuscript if this is what he/she wants.

Some editors prefer that the author submit novels in completed form. Check the market directories or write the publisher to determine what his preference is.

Short material, such as brief articles (under 500 words), and short stories of any length, need not be preceded by a query. Send the complete, final draft of the manuscript.

Always query about a non-fiction book, although in some case editors prefer an outline along with the query.

While a query letter should always be an original, sample chapters, outlines, plot summaries, proposals, etc., can be machine copies, providing they are clean, readable copies.

It is not considered ethical to submit complete manuscripts to several publishers simultaneously, but there is no objection to simultaneous submissions of queries and outlines.

The Business of Writing

One of the less exciting aspects of writing, but also one of the more essential for the professional, is record-keeping. This includes a record of your expenses and income as well as a travelogue of your manuscripts—where they have gone, when they were returned, comments about them from editors, and the payment received for them.

A careful record of your expenses vs. income is important not only so that you will know whether your writing is a profitable business or merely an expensive hobby, but also to keep in good standing with the Internal Revenue Service.

Keeping track of your manuscripts is equally important. A professional writer may have a dozen or so articles or stories in the mail at any one time and should he/she depend on memory alone there is the danger of resubmitting a manuscript to an editor who has already rejected it, or possibly submitting a manuscript to a pubishing house when it has already been accepted by another.

Of tremendous help to the writer are the comments that may be received from an editor even when the manuscript is being rejected. Such comments should be a part of the manuscript log.

We've included in this chapter a pay formula that may be of value once you are obtaining writing assignments from editors. This pay formula is also helpful if an organization requests you to prepare a newsletter for them or should you become involved in some other writing project—collaboration, ghostwriting, a public relations release, etc.

The section on "Income Tax and the Writer" will provide some general guidelines as to allowable deductions and qualifications necessary to be considered a professional writer. However, income tax laws change frequently and it is wise to discuss your tax problems with an accountant.

PAY SCHEDULE FOR WRITERS

At least five factors influence the rates paid a professional writer.

First, the client (editor, publisher, advertising or public relations director) needs a man or woman who knows the industry and interests of the client and client's readers or customers. The writer selected should know the special field of interest well and have experience in writing about it. Such special experience or background may range from engineering and scientific knowledge to the fine points of artistic performance and expression and the general principles of sound business management.

The large majority of truly professional writers talk to persons in any given field with full knowledge of the special language of that discipline or field. They acquaint their potential clients with the extent of their knowledge and background in such fields, and when they approach new fields of knowledge may accept a lower rate of compensation for their initial efforts in such an area.

Second, the amount paid for a given piece of writing must reflect the type of output desired. Professional writers may work at three or more levels, not reflecting degrees of competence or excellence, but varieties of function and refinement that must be applied in the process from raw research and interview to production of the finished presentation, in whatever form that takes.

For example, the writer may be asked to work as a 'legman,' to use an old journalistic term, or even virtually a detective, gathering facts for staff editors to rewrite. He or she acts as sort of a human tape-recorder, but with discretion and professional screening and interpretation added to the raw data.

At another level, as a 'reporter,' the writer gets the facts, and writes straight, well-organized copy, properly documented and with only moderate editing needed. Accuracy is verified as necessary.

If a writer is to produce 'finished' writing, he or she supplies finely composed articles or other material virtually ready to present to readers or other audiences for the client. The work matches the publication's or client's style. Technical precision and sensitivity to reader and client needs and orientation are essential to a well-produced piece at this level.

The writer may further be called upon to aid in the production and utilization of the material he or she has written, by providing design, illustration and marketing counsel and services.

Each further function, refinement and service provided in conjunction with the original research and raw fact gathering will demand more hours—and many times, a multiplicity of professioinal skills—than the same amount of material would require in basic reportage. Consequently, each level of service provided should merit higher pay for the same published length.

Third, a writer's pay should reflect not only the time involved in producing the client's writing requirements, but also the overhead time involved in operating a business. A survey by the Associated Business Writers of America (ABWA) shows that its members average 40 percent of their time in the field, 40 percent at the typewriter, word processor, or tape recorder, and 20 percent in overhead work—answering letters, amending proposals to prospective clients, procuring writing supplies, billing and paying bills. That is as much a part of the writer's costs—and as unavoidable a factor in serving clients and editors—as is the cost of driving from Point X to Point Z to gather information on the customer's behalf.

Fourth, as an independent business person, the freelancer must pay for the expenses of a place to work (even if a portion of his or her own home), equipment, supplies, travel and other work-related expense. $500 paid to a freelancer may only be half or less net income after these expenses are deducted. The ABWA survey showed these ranging from 80 percent of gross income (for a writer with his own staff) to 40 percent for a solo writer who spends no more than bus fare for travel and processes photos and retypes manuscripts in his or her home without outside help. An important consideration is that all these expenses and costs occur for a writer before a manuscript or other written work is seen by a client or editor. A freelancer needs at least $4,000 working capital for current business expenses, even if payment from editors and other clients is prompt, perhaps on delivery of the completed work.

Word and page and other 'piece-work' rates of payment for writers are generally unfair and too simplistic to be adequate gauges of the effort involved. While some writers work more rapidly than others in one or another phase of the work, those arbitrary measures usually fail to recognize the time devoted to the assignment, the skill of the writer, and the required degree of expertise in the field.

Fifth, and finally, keep in mind that the freelance writer working on behalf of the editor, publisher or other client in the field represents that client almost as strongly as a full-time member of the client's staff. Both the writer and the client know the relationship is that of an independent contract, but the freelancer still projects and extends the client's image. That's worth something, too.

It's important to editors, publishers and other clients to be represented capably and wholeheartedly by a mature, qualified professional writer, the same kind of person one might proudly identify as a regular member of the company staff. It is equally important for a writer to know he or she is being fairly compensated to deliver a satisfactory, thoroughly professional and on-time piece of work.

The Freelance Writer's Pay Formula

How to figure fair payment for a writer is essential information, not only for editors, but for the writer as well. This formula, developed by ABWA, is quite easy to use, although it doesn't fit all circumstances. It does, however, provide an acceptable basis for negotiating.

The "ABWA Pay Formula" has five steps:

(1) Determine what annual salary this writer might earn in a staff position.

(2) Divide the annual salary by 2,000 to obtain a net hourly wage.

(3) Double the hourly wage to cover the writer's direct and overhead expenses. This gives a gross hourly rate.

(4) Increase the gross hourly rate by 25%, to cover overhead time. This is the billing rate.

(5) Multiply the billing rate by total productive hours, to arrive at fair payment for an assignment.

For example: An editor considers the writer is capable of earning $10,000 annually. Divide this figure by 2,000. The result is $5 net hourly wage.

Doubling the $5 net wage makes the gross hourly rate of $10. (A short cut is to divide $10,000 by 1,000, which gives the gross hourly wage directly and is easy to remember.) One-fourth of this amount for overhead time is $2.50. Added to $10 this establishes $12.50 as the hourly billing rate.

The editor's assignment involves two days' production time - travel, interview, photography and writing. Two eight-hour days total 16 hours, which multiplied by $12.50 equals a fair payment of $200, for a writer of this caliber on the job.

Here are some sample rate structures:

Net Annual Income	Net Weekly Wage	Net Hourly Wage	Gross Hourly Rate	Hourly Billing Rate
$10,000	$200	$5.00	$10.00	$12.50
12,000	240	6.00	12.00	15.00
15,000	300	7.50	15.00	18.75
20,000	400	10.00	20.00	25.00
25,000	500	12.50	25.00	31.25
30,000	600	15.00	30.00	37.50
40,000	800	20.00	40.00	50.00
50,000	1,000	25.00	50.00	62.50

A writer *may* use several billing rates. As a specialist, he may be worth $25.00 hourly at consulting and research. Reportage in his specialty could run $18.75 per hour. For reporting in less familiar areas, this same writer might ask only $12.50 an hour.

We assume the client isn't shopping without regard for competence or impression made on the person interviewed. With minimal red-tape, the writer augments the client's staff for a brief period. Yet he or she should measure up to staff standards, in competence and in projecting the company image.

Payment as expressed in the formula means everything—fees, advances, bonuses, expenses. The latter are properly included because they usually are proportionate to fees. For instance, a client doesn't invest in a 7,000 mile roundtrip for a cub reporter.

Net hourly wage is what the writer pays income tax on, after all business expense deductions. It compares to a staff writer's take-home pay.

Gross hourly rate is important because ABWA surveys show half a writer's total income goes to direct and overhead expenses (exclusive of long distance travel). This does include, however, fringe benefits such as the two weeks vacation omitted above. Fringes in publishing usually add 20% or more to a staff member's salary, says U.S. Chamber of Commerce.

Productive hours are those spent directly on interviews, research, writing, photography, travel. Productive travel time is door-to-door, except for personal time spent in normal pursuits (TV, reading, etc.).

Overhead work is *non*-productive hours not attributable to specific jobs. For every four hours of interview, writing or travel, one hour or more goes into "overhead work"—queries, negotiations, correspondence, phoning, bookkeeping, tax work, planning, purchasing, mailing, filing, maintenance.

Publishing houses use secretaries, typists, clerks, bookkeepers, and various artisans for such work. And their wages are charged to editorial budgets, or to the administrative overhead included in editorial costs.

To compensate a writer for overhead time then, it is pro- rated to productive hours. That is, gross hourly rate is increased by one-fourth to compile the actual billing rate.

For the mathematically inclined, all the above is condensed in an algebraic equation. F = total payment or fee; H = the number of productive hours; W = net hourly wage:

$$F = H(2W + {}^{2W}/_4)$$

Short jobs deserve higher billing rates. A long assignment may warrant slightly lower billing rates. Some overhead work is the same for a $50 job as for a $500 assignment. But that's where negotiating begins.

THE FREELANCER'S BOOKKEEPING SYSTEM

Accurate and complete records are necessary to prove your tax liability to the IRS.

> Regardless of the bookkeeping system you use, your records must be permanent, accurate, complete, and must clearly establish income, deductions, credits, employee information, etc. The law does not require any particular kind of records.

> Books and records of your business must be available at all times for inspection by Internal Revenue officers.

> Records supporting items on a tax return should be retained until the statute of limitations for that return expires. However, in many cases, the taxpayer should retain all records indefinitely.

These statements establish the need for developing a good bookkeeping system, no matter how small or large your business may be. Since a freelancer's tax returns already are suspect, inadequate records of receipts and expenditures can be a disaster should the return be audited.

The need for accuracy and completeness is almost self- explanatory. Every dollar received or spent to maintain the operation should be recorded to show the amount, the source of a payment received, the recipients of expenditures paid out, the reason for an expenditure, and the type of proof (receipt, check, credit card, etc.). It is necessary to be able to prove expenses listed as deductions, so some form of written proof should be available.

The requirement for permanent records makes it necessary to follow certain procedures. First, the record book should be permanently bound in such a manner that pages cannot be removed easily. Looseleaf notebooks or pads of paper do not constitute appropriate records. Most office-supply stores stock a variety of record-keeping books, the best of which use a two-page spread for each calendar week.

Initially you may obtain a bound notebook and prepare your own ledger, similar to the sample shown in this chapter. It is important to keep copies of your receipts in addition to making entries in a ledger. Permanent records must be recorded in ink. Pencil entries are not acceptable in an IRS audit. Erasures are not acceptable either; corrections should be made by crossing out the erroneous entry with a single line, not by obliterating the entry with a covering of ink or correction fluid. Corrections made by erasure or complete obliteration are highly suspect in any audit.

As you become more successful and your writing business more complicated, you may decide to use either single or double-entry bookkeeping. The single-entry system is the simplest method and is the one most often used by free-lancers and other small businesses. However, it lacks the built-in checks and balances that are found in the double-entry system.

Nevertheless, double-entry bookkeeping can be a real burden because of its complexity, and it usually shows up only in corporate business structures where there are needs for recording more complex information.

Single-entry bookkeeping is a partially complete system of accounts in that it usually concentrates only on the profit and loss statement and not the balance sheet. While this system has its limitations, it may be used effectively by one starting out in a small business. A single-entry system can be a relatively simple one, which records the flow of income and expense. Through the use of a daily summary of cash receipts, a monthly summary of receipts, and a monthly disbursements journal, this system can be used to record income and expenses adequately for tax purposes.

Double-entry bookkeeping usually is the preferable method for business records. This system makes use of journals and ledgers; transactions are entered first in a journal, and then summary totals of the transactions (usually monthly) are posted to the appropriate ledger accounts. Ledger accounts are of five types: income, expenses, asset, liability, and net worth. Income and expense accounts are closed on the basis of the annual accounting period; asset, liability, and net worth accounts are maintained on a permanent basis.

Few free-lancers have the time or inclination to deal with double-entry bookkeeping unless they hire a CPA. The single- entry system is simple enough for most individuals to handle themselves, and the weekly bookkeeping record already described is an easy method of maintaining adequate single-entry records.

YOUR WRITING INCOME

Date	Source	Manuscript	Amount	Comments

YOUR WRITING EXPENSES

Date	Paid To	Description	Amount	Comments

YOUR MANUSCRIPT LOG

Date Sent	Manuscript Title	To	Date Accepted or Rejected	Payment	Comments

INCOME TAX AND THE WRITER

(Adapted from a report by Paul A. Luers & Associates)

Note: Due to constantly changing tax laws, the following information should be used to provide general guidelines only. It is recommended that a professional accountant or tax expert be consulted.

Writing, if pursued with a profit motive, constitutes a business, the income or loss from which is required to be reported on the writer's income tax return. Gross income is generally readily identifiable as it is normally received as checks representing an advance or royalties or a payment for a literary composition. Expenses, on the other hand, are not so easily identified.

The 1986 Tax Reform Act required writers to capitalize the expenses associated with writing where there was no related income in a given year at a rate of 50 percent for the first year and 25 percent for each succeeding year. The 1988 act exempts authors, artists, photographers from the uniform capitalization rules effective for costs incurred after 1986.

Hobby loss rules have been expanded within the Tax Reform Act of 1986. The new rules require the activity to be profitable in three out of five consecutive years. This rule requires that a profit be shown in the initial year. Therefore, if you are just starting a writing business and incurred losses for the initial year or two you might be barred from taking those losses in the current year.

Home office deductions can only be taken to the extent that there is net income from your business as a writer. Income or loss is calculated after all the business expenses are deducted, including the home office deductions. If in the case of a loss, home office deductions are reduced to the extent that the loss is eliminated.

If the writer maintains a separate room or area in his home for writing, an allocable share of the home expenses such as rent, utlities, depreciation, insurance, repairs, taxes, and interest qualify as deductions. The percentage of business expenses which qualify are computed using a formula based on the amount of business square footage compared to the total. The business use of the office must be exlusively "for writing" and utilized on a regular basis.

Travel, meals and entertainment expenses were modified under the 1986 law, as follows:

Fully deductible—
    Business travel
    Meals at qualified banquet meetings
    Food and beverages at company parties, workshops
    Small business gifts of food or beverages

80 percent deductible—
  Business entertainment
  Business meals, including taxes and tips
  Business meals that are a part of overnight business travel
Not deductible—
  Any portion of a business meal that is "lavish and extravagant"
  Expenses connected with attending investment seminars
  Travel as a form of education

You must be able to substantiate all expenses in order to deduct them. The date, place, amount of expense, the business purpose and the names of any business relationships of parties involved must all be documented. The law further requires that substantial business discussions must be held directly before, during, or after any business meal or entertainment.

Automobile expenses can be deducted using one of two methods of calculations. The first is taking the actual business mileage at 24 cents per mile for the first 15,000 miles and 11 cents per mile for business miles in excess of 15,000. The 11 cents a mile rate must be used after the taxpayer has taken the highest mileage base deductions allowable for the car for 60,000 business miles (or the car has otherwise been fully depreciated). The second method involves relating the percentage of business miles to the total mileage, times the actual expenses of operating a vehicle. Such expenses include fuel, oil, repairs, insurance, licenses, tires, sales taxes, interest, and depreciation. Adequate records must be kept.

When taking automobile expenses the taxpayer must disclose on his tax return the total business, commuting and other personal mileage, along with the percentage of business use, date the automobile was placed in service, use of another vehicle, whether or not the taxpayer has evidence and, if so, whether that evidence is written.

Computers also have restrictions. Logs must be maintained showing the business portion of a computer. Less than a 50 percent usage restricts your deductions. The life of a computer has been extended from five to seven years, thus reducing the deduction on a year-by-year basis.

Other deductible expenses may include:

Critique fees	Legal and accounting
Manuscript evaluation	Depreciation of business assets
Office supplies	Printing
Insurance	Repairs
Interest on business assets	Secretarial expenses
Taxes	Telephone
Seminars	Utilities
Travel & Entertainment	Office expenses
Typing and Copying costs	Postage

The Taxpayer's Bill of Rights

The Technical and Miscellaneous Revenue Act of 1988 includes certain rights given to taxpayers. Some of the provisions are:

IRS must send a statement clearly stating the taxpayer's rights and the IRS's obligations before starting audit, appeals, refund and collection procedures.

IRS must issue regulations setting up standards for selection of a time and place for interviewing a taxpayer.

The IRS must withdraw penalties or additions to tax attributable to incorrect advice furnished to the taxpayer in writing by the IRS.

IRS must wait 30 days from the date of written notice to the date of collecting tax by levy.

Taxpayers are given the right to sue if the IRS recklessly or intentionally disregards the code or regulations in connection with the collection of tax.

Here are TWO FINAL SUGGESTIONS: (1) Establish a separate business bank account to conduct your writing business. This will simplify the recordkeeping which will be necessary to accurately determine your annual income. (2) As this report is limited in income tax considerations, anyone embarking on or involved in a writing career should engage a professional accountant or tax expert who can advise you on your special tax situation.

The Legal Side of Writing

HIGHLIGHTS OF THE COPYRIGHT LAW

(By David A. Weinstein, Denver attorney specializing in
trademark, copyright, entertainment and art-related matters.)

COPYRIGHT—PAST AND PRESENT

On October 19, 1976, Public Law 94-553 was signed by Gerald Ford. This
law put an end to the Copyright Act of 1909 and gave us a new Copyright
Law that, for all practical purposes, became effective January 1, 1978.

For years to come there will likely be lawsuits and court disputes to
resolve questions and clarify or interpret the language of the bill. But despite
the gray areas, the new law clearly provides writers with a number of
advantages they did not have in the past, and denies publishers some of the
inherent rights they claimed under the previous law.

Whereas before, authors often sold all rights to magazines without
realizing they did so (mainly because it was up to the author to state what
rights he was selling lest it be assumed all rights were sold) it is now the
opposite. The magazine must state, in writing, what rights it is buying; if a
particular right is not mentioned in this statement, it remains with the
author. Book contracts continue to specify rights.

Under the 1976 law a single system of statutory copyright protection
extends for both published *and unpublished* works from the moment of their
creation. (Creation here means the moment the work is in a fixed, tangible or
nontransitory form; in the case of unpublished or yet-to-be-published
manuscripts, this would mean the final draft or final copy.) The old law
provided for common law copyright for unpublished works, and statutory
copyright for works when published. This new system significantly reduces
the importance of publication and grants, from the beginning, power of
copyright to the author. It also puts us more in harmony with other nations
in the world that have a similar single system of copyright protection from
the moment of a work's creation.

The 1976 law also included a manufacturing clause which does away with some of the restrictions and disadvantages regarding publication in foreign countries. In contrast to the old law, copyright protection is no longer denied protection for works first published abroad.

Librarians, teachers and others involved in distributing information taken from copyrighted material, are much more limited in their duplicating privileges.

Duration Of Copyright

The present law gives a writer copyright protection for his/her life plus 50 years. Beyond this term there is no provision for renewal. In the event of any ambiguity or dispute about a particular author's death, copyright discontinues 75 years from the year of publication of a work or 100 years from its creation, depending on which happens first.

Where works made-for-hire and anonymous and pseudonymous works are concerned, the copyright term is also 75 years from publication or 100 years from creation, whichever occurs first. This doesn't apply to a pseudonymous work when the author's identity is recorded with the Copyright Office.

Works that were copyrighted prior to January 1, 1978 and have not been renewed may be renewed (after the initial 28 years) for 47 more years. Copyrights that have already been renewed before January 1, 1978 are extended to last a total term of 75 years beyond the date they were originally secured.

Anything that fell into the public domain before January 1, 1978 remains so. Likewise, no provision is made for restoring protection to works that lost their copyrights in the past, regardless of the reason for loss.

Any work which is eligible for copyright and created on or after January 1, 1978 is entitled to the life-plus-50-year term already mentioned. Co-authored works are granted a term lasting 50 years after the death of the last surviving author.

Unpublished manuscripts, no matter when or if they are ever published, are protected for the same life-plus-50 or 75/100-year terms applicable to new works. This is true for unpublished works created both before and after January 1, 1978 and is one of the most important changes in the 1976 law. In the case of unpublished works created before January 1, 1978, protection is guaranteed for a minimum of 25 years past that date, regardless of when the work was created.

All copyrights last until the end of the calendar year in which they would otherwise expire. If a copyright went into effect on March 4, 1990, it would extend until December 31 (not March 4) of that fiftieth year after the author's demise or the seventy-fifth year after publication, etc.

Definition And Ownership Of Copyright

Copyright is generally defined as protection of ownership guaranteed by federal law to authors of literary, dramatic and other kinds of intellectual creations. This protection helps insure the author against infringement or piracy of his work and grants him certain exclusive (though not unlimited) rights in such works. The owner of the copyright is given the right to: 1) reproduce the work in copies; 2) prepare derivative works based on the original; 3) distribute to the public copies of the work by sale or other transfer of ownership or by rental, lease or lending; 4) perform publicly a literary, dramatic or audiovisual work and 5) display publicly such a work.

Copyright for magazine or anthology contributions remain with you, the writer, unless you've agreed *in writing* to sell or transfer copyright ownership to the publisher of the magazine or anthology. The publisher cannot use the contributed article, story, etc., a second time, without obtaining further permission from the author—unless the use of the work is in a future revised edition or in future issues of the same issue of the magazine or anthology in which the work originally appeared.

Even though a work is published with the copyright notice in the publisher's name, the author remains the owner.

Written agreements are highly advisable from the publisher's standpoint. Permission to publish should be given by the author in writing and this should have the author's signature. A short personal letter will often be enough but be sure the letter spells out the specific rights being granted the publisher. Without a letter or contract, you could well be inadvertently inviting the publisher to attempt to use more rights than he is allowed. Likewise, without a letter or contract, the publisher is at risk not having anything to rely upon with respect to the extent of the license given by the author.

A work "made-for-hire" is one written by a writer while employed by someone else. Such a work is created by the writer within the writer's scope of employment by the employer. The copyright in this case belongs to the employer and not the writer. The latter does not necessarily have to be a full-time employee of the business and no written agreement is required. House organs may fall under this category.

A Supreme Court decision in 1989 clarified some of the provisions of the work-for-hire portion of the copyright law, and amendments to this section of the 1976 law will probably be enacted in the future.

A foreword written by one author for the purpose of introducing, praising, etc., another author's work may also be a work made-for-hire whose copyright belongs to the author of the original work, provided a written agreement to this effect between the author of the foreword and the author of the broader work has been made beforehand.

The 1976 law is very specific in its redefinition of divisible copyrights (first and second serial, book, foreign, etc.). "Any of the exclusive rights comprised in a copyright, including any subdivision of any of [those] rights may be transferred...and owned separately." This means that each right may be handled separately. The writer has the right to divide up a copyright in the most remunerative way and retain for future bargaining any rights s/he does not wish to include in a transfer.

The most important point for freelancers to remember is that it should no longer be necessary to indicate what rights you are selling, since, normally, you would be selling first publication rights only. Be careful not to use the phrase "all rights" if an author does not intend to transfer all of the rights of copyright. Whatever rights a publisher buys, s/he must indicate in writing what those rights are. If the agreement does not state a certain right, the author did not sell it.

The ownership of copyright, or of any exclusive rights in a copyright, is distinguished from ownership of a material object in which the work is embodied. An author may sell to a publisher the right to print, distribute and sell for profit copies of a particular work but the author retains copyright on the original manuscript and in 35 years the right or rights s/he sold to the publisher may revert to him/her. Reversion is not automatic. The author must follow the procedure outlined in the statute to effect a reversion.

Notice, Deposit And Registration

On March 1, 1989 significant amendments to the 1976 law were made. One change eliminates the requirement that a copyright notice be placed on publicly distributed copies of protected material. However, authors are urged to place the copyright notice on their work, whether published or not. This does not entail that much trouble and there is nothing to lose by doing so. Another amendment of importance enables the U.S. to become a party to the Berne Convention for the Protection of Literary and Artistic works. It gives American copyright owners the right to receive automatically legal protection for their works in many foreign countries.

Any contract drawn up with a publisher should include a provision that the proper copyright notice has to appear in all copies of the work distributed. As long as such a provision is in the contract, any errors or omissions in the notice will not invalidate the author's copyright—even if the error or omission is not corrected.

The following three elements constitute copyright notice:

1) the symbol © or the word "Copyright," or the abbreviation "Copr."
2) the year of first publication of the work or, if unpublished, date of creation.
3) the name of the owner of copyright in the work, or an abbreviation of which the name can be recognized, or a generally known designation of the owner.

The act of "publication," as defined in the copyright act, occurs when copies of a work are distributed to the public by sale or other transfer of ownership, or by rental, lease, or lending. The offering to distribute copies to a group of persons for purposes of further distribution, public performance, or public display, also constitutes publication.

Whereas the previous law stipulated exact location where the notice should appear on books and other printed publications, the new law simply requires that the notice be placed in such a way and such a location as to give reasonable notice of the copyright claim. It should be "visually perceptible." However, somewhere on the title page, below your by-line, say, in the case of unpublished manuscripts, or on the credits page in a published book, are still the best locations.

In the case of collective works, a single article, story or poem in a magazine or anthology, etc., may bear its own copyright notice. Or the collective work as a whole may bear a single notice and all the material within the work will be protected regardless of whether or not individual contributions bear a notice. Each contribution's copyright, however, will remain with the author. Again, it is advisable that you see that your work bears its own notice, the "liberality" of the new law notwithstanding. That liberality will no doubt be tested by editors and publishers alike and it is wise for the writer to take every precaution s/he can.

If an author is registering a group of contributions on his/her own, individual notices are needed on each contribution. This does not apply for group *renewal* registration, however.

Section 408, subsection (c) contains a clause stating: "the Register of Copyrights shall establish regulations specifically permitting a single registration for a group of works by the same individual author, all first pubished as contributions to periodicals, including newspapers, within a twelve-month period, on the basis of a single deposit, application and registration fee... if...A) each of the works as first published bore a separate copyright notice, and the name of the owner in the work...; and B) if the deposit consists of one copy of the entire issue of the periodical, or of the entire section in the cause of a newspaper, in which each contribution was first published; and C) if the application identifies each work separately, including the periodical containing it and its date of first publication." In other words, provided the above stipulations are observed, any number of stories, articles, etc., published in a single magazine during a twelve-month period, may be covered by one registration, deposit and fee.

No later than three months after publication of a work, you should, for full protection, deposit with the Copyright Office two complete copies of the "best edition" of the work being registered. "Best edition" means "the edition, published in the United States at any time before the date of deposit, that the Library of Congress determines to be most suitable for its purposes."

While registration is not absolutely necessary for copyright protection, it should be remembered that *a work must be registered in order to sue for infringement*. The registration procedure involves depositing with the Copyright Office in Washington, DC, the required number of copies, an application and a fee. Deposit requirements are:

1) one complete copy in the case of an unpublished work
2) two complete copies of the best edition of a published work
3) one complete copy of a work first published outside the US as so published
4) or one complete copy of the best edition of the collective work for a contribution to a collective work.

When you are ready to register a work, you must file an application for registration by the Copyright Office (types of forms are listed on next page). The form will ask for:

1) name and address of the copyright claimant (you).
2) for works other than anonymous or pseudonymous works, the name and nationality or domicile of the author and date of death of any deceased author.
3) for anonymous or pseudonymous works, the nationality or domicile of the author or authors.
4) for a work made-for-hire, a statement to that effect.
5) if the claimant is not the author, a brief statement of how the claimant obtained ownership of the copyright.
6) the title of the work and any other former or alternative titles under which the work can be identified.
7) the year in which creation of the work was completed.
8) if the work has been published, the date and nation of its first publication.
9) for compilations or derivative works, an identification of any pre-existing work or works on which it is based or which it incorporates and a brief statement of additional material covered by the copyright claim being registered.
10) any other information required by the Register of Copyrights as bearing on the preparation or identification of the work or the existence, ownership or duration of the copyright.

Note: the Register may or may not accept a claim for registration. If the application is denied, the Register will send the applicant an explanation as to why.

Under the present law the work must be deposited with the Library of Congress *after publicaton* while the registration is basically voluntary. The requirement of two copies for deposit in the case of a published work is necessary for the separate purposes of copyright registration and LC deposit.

Registration Forms And Fees

When applying for registration, the Copyright Office advises that you send payment in the form of a check, money order or bank draft made out to: *Register of Copyrights*. The Copyright Office says it will assume no responsibility for loss of payment sent in the form of currency. If registration materials are sent from outside the US, arrangements should be made for remittances to be immediately payable in US greenbacks.

Copies of the necessary forms can be obtained from the Copyright Office free of charge.

Whether the registration is made by the author or by a transferee of an exclusive right (e.g., a publisher), the author should be noted as the "Copyright Claimant." If the work has been made-for-hire, however, or if the author has transferred ownership of the copyright, s/he would, of course, not be listed as the claimant.

The majority of applications will have to be submitted on one of the five basic forms. Detailed instructions on the registration procedure and its requirements are given on the forms.

Form TX	for all types of published/unpublished nondramatic literary works (works written in words or other verbal or numerical symbols) such as fiction, nonfiction, poetry, periodicals, textbooks, etc. TX stands for "text."
Form PA	for all published/unpublished works of the performing arts (works performed before an audience) such as dramatic, musical or audiovisual works.
Form VA	for works of the visual arts such as "pictorial, graphic, or sculptural works."
Form SR	for sound recordings.
Form RE	for renewal registration of copyright claim on works already in their first term on January 1, 1978. This claim applies to all renewal registrations, regardless of the class in which the original registration was made (i.e., before January 1, 1978).
Form CA	for supplementary registration; to be used to correct an error in a previous registration or to clarify or amplify the information contained in a registration.
Form GR/CP	for group registration for contributions to periodicals; this should be used in conjunction with one of the five basic forms (e.g., if the work being registered is a group of short stories published in a magazine within a twelve-month period, Form TX would be the basic form required and Form GR/CP would be needed as an adjunct).

Members should send requests for specific forms, stating the kind of form you need, to: Information and Publications Section, Copyright Office, Library of Congress, Washington, DC 20559. In this request, state if the work is published or unpublished.

Registration Fees: (All fees subject to change)

For each registration	$10.00
Renewals	$ 6.00
Receipt of Deposits	$ 2.00

Additional fees are charged when the occasion warrants them— for other services such as certifications, recordations, searches, etc. The Copyright Office will send you detailed information on all aspects of forms, fees and so forth. This is available free of charge upon request.

Limitations On Exclusive Rights—Or "Fair Use"

A student, teacher or librarian may duplicate copyrighted works for limited uses in classwork, research and other kinds of information gathering and distribution as long as the duplicated copies fall within the limits of "brevity, spontaneity, lack of cumulative effect and inclusion on copies of a copyright notice." Limited uses of copyrighted material for the purposes of criticism, comment, news reporting, etc., also come within this provision of "fair use" and, as long as those who use the material abide by the required guidelines (set forth in the statute), such use does not constitute infringement of the author's rights.

This doctrine of "fair use" has been one of the most controversial issues related to copyright law since 1909, especially in the last two or three decades when so many effective ways of duplication of printed matter have come on the scene. The definition and guidelines governing fair use in the new law are a result of many courtroom disputes which took this issue to task. Though courtroom wrangles will no doubt continue, the unlimited and wholesale duplication of copyrighted material by people involved in the distribution of an author's work (for varying reasons) that has prevailed in the past, has been seriously curbed.

The 1976 law gives the following guidelines for determining "fair use."

1) the purpose and character of the use, including whether the use is of a commercial nature or is for nonprofit educational purposes
2) the nature of the copyrighted work
3) the effect of the use on the potential market for, or the value of, the copyrighted work
4) the amount and substantiality of the portion used in relation to the copyrighted work.

What Cannot Be Copyrighted

The 1976 law does not give copyright protection to any "idea, procedure, process, system, method of operation, concept, principle, or discovery, regardless of the form in which it is described, explained, illustrated or embodied in a work."

Established facts and statistics are in the public domain and may be excerpted from a copyrighted work and used without permission. Warning: if unusual or little-known facts are published in such a way as to be unique to the author, that particular style or method is inviolable. Only the facts may be used.

Most copyright owners have not objected, in the past, to the use of a few words (usually up to 50 for the purpose of quoting, etc., or up to 500 in the case of reviews) from a copyrighted work unless this constitutes a significant part of the work (say a complete short poem, for example). To use longer quotations, or if in doubt, write the publisher, detail exactly what you wish to use, and request permission. Even though the work is copyrighted in the author's name, it is still preferable to write the publisher. If s/he doesn't have the rights, s/he can provide you with the address of the author. Whether payment will be required depends upon the use and other circumstances.

A title cannot be copyrighted. However, if a title has a unique quality or gains a wide acceptance, the author may claim a special equity in it and claim infringement if any unauthorized use is made of it. For example, *Life Begins At Forty* became very popular. When an advertiser used it to sell a product, the author sued, claiming that he had given it a special meaning and that it was his property. Certain titles may be protected under the area of law dealing with trademarks.

For all practical purposes, many publications of the United States Government are in the public domain. These are usually works prepared by an officer or employee of the US Government as part of that person's official, job-related duties. Looked at another way, you could say that something written by an officer or employee of the US government as part of that person's official duties is a work made-for-hire and the employer, being the Government, is you, John Q. Citizen.

Copies of the copyright statute are available free of charge by writing to the Copyright Office, Library of Congress, Washington, DC 20559. Your name can be added to the Copyright Office Mailing List by sending a written request to the above address.

LITERARY RIGHTS

Until the early part of the twentieth century, few markets existed to which freelance writers could sell their work. The diversity of technological innovations, the cross-pollination of cultures, and the continual spread of a complex and multi- interest world, however, have brought about many new channels and outlets for the work of writers and increased the number of potentially different ways whereby such work may be sold.

The new copyright law that went into effect January 1, 1978 is, to a large degree, a result of this new diversity of market potential. In the past, it was virtually standard practice for a magazine—and until recent decades, a book publisher—to buy all rights to a work. Such procedure was not necessarily a consequence of the publisher's desire to fleece the writer, but often a consequence of neither publisher or writer being aware of any subsidiary markets; so neither thought in terms of subsidiary rights inhering in a work.

With the appearance of more and more magazines, each one growing increasingly slanted toward a particular audience of readers, the advent of the paperback, the motion picture, radio, television, foreign publishers wanting to buy American literature for their readers abroad, etc., subsidiary or secondary markets multiplied. The most recent example of this expansion of market potential can be seen in the area of what is called 'merchandising rights.' Such items as T-shirts, toys, games, and the like, derived from a popular TV show or movie—which, in turn are often derived from a novel or play—may be schlock to the cognoscenti but they can mean added royalties to the novelist or playwright whose work they exploit.

Selling And Retaining Rights

Though some publishers are trying to operate as they have in the past, i.e., attempting to buy all rights, the present copyright law explicitly states that a written agreement should be manifest between author and publisher and should spell out what rights are being sold and what rights retained by the author.

Notes in market directories (such as *Writer's Market* or *The Writer's Handbook*), in writers' magazines, masthead notices at the front of magazines which state the publisher buys all rights, *do not constitute written agreements between author and publisher*. Unless there is such a written agreement (signed by both author and publisher), it is to be assumed the writer is selling only the following nonexclusive rights: (1) to use the particular piece being bought in the collective work for which it is intended—i.e., the particular issue of magazine or anthology; (2) to use the contribution in later collective works in the same series; and (3) to use it in revisions of that specific collective work. For example, a magazine that buys the piece may have the right to run it again in a later issue of that same magazine without additional compensation to the author. This is one of the reasons the author should insist on that written agreement which spells out exactly what rights are being sold and, to prevent a situation like the one outlined above, the author should make sure the publisher is buying only *First Serial Rights*, or *First North American Serial Rights* (definitions will be gone into below).

The unknown writer, or one without a substantial track record, is usually in a poor bargaining position when it comes to haggling over rights. The publisher may adopt a 'take it or leave it' attitude; either it buys all rights or it buys nothing. In such a case, the writer must decide what is best, must weigh the advantages and disadvantages of such an agreement. If, for instance, a magazine article has little market potential beyond the magazine offering to buy it only under the all-rights stipulation, any contention could well be superfluous. Or, if it is a case of a writer's first sale, then it could be worth that first publishing credit for the writer to bow to the publisher's will.

Often, though, publishers will give in if the writer simply makes it known he or she is cognizant of his/her rights. And in many cases where a magazine insists on initial purchase of all rights, it will revert reprint or secondary rights to the author after an appropriate period (usually about a year after original publication) upon the author's request. There isn't any particular form required for requesting reassignment of rights; a simple note to the publisher, or editor, asking that the rights revert to you, pointing out the date of original sale and publication of the piece, etc., should suffice.

Many writers remain inadequately informed regarding what rights they have in a given work and what rights are salable in the literary marketplace. The names of rights are sometimes confusing, misleading, or too abstract for for those not well versed in the area to fully understand. The following list of rights and their definitions should help clarify and elucidate terms and concepts.

Magazine Rights

All Rights: This is probably the most self-explanatory of terms relating to literary rights and it denotes the least desirable of arrangements for the writer. It refers to every right belonging to a work and if the writer sells all rights, s/he is selling the work completely to the purchaser buying those rights. The writer may not use the work in any way again (in the form in which it was sold) and the purchaser, the publisher, may use it as many times as it wishes, without paying the author an additional dime for that use.

There are some agreements, and book contracts, that read like a document drafted by Mephistopheles. These state the publisher is, for all practical purposes, buying all rights forever and throughout the universe. In the case of some book contracts, there may be an option clause that could mean the writer is also committed to selling future work to this same publisher *in perpetuum.* Option clauses, like everything else in a contract, should be read very carefully and if the writer does not understand a clause, phrase, etc., he should seek professional advice. An option clause that would commit a writer's next work to the publisher *in perpetuum* should *always* be eliminated from the contract, no matter what the situation may be and if the publisher refuses, the writer should take the work elsewhere.

In the event the publisher refuses to negotiate, or make changes, in an all-rights agreement, the writer must decide whether it is or is not advantageous to sign. As stated above, if there is little chance of the work finding a reprint or subsidiary market, signing could be acceptable since, in such a case, *all rights* has little relevance. But one never knows what may develop in the way of markets, next day or next year, and it is wise to fight against an agreement of this type if possible, and at least try to have it written in that subsidiary rights will be returned to the author after an appropriate period has elapsed since original publication.

First Serial Rights: This does not refer to the 'serial' rights in the sense of serialization in a magazine. The word 'serial' here refers to the serial or periodical issue of a publication. If you sell 'first serial rights,' you are selling to a publication the right to use the article or story for the first time in print and no other periodical (magazine) may use it until the purchaser of First Rights has published it. After the publisher buying First Rights has run the piece, you are free to sell it for reprint, or other secondary rights.

First Rights: Refers to the right to use a work for the first time in whatever publishing medium the purchaser desires.

First North American Serial Rights: Refers to the right to publish a work for the first time in a magazine or periodical whose principal circulation area and whose offices are in North America. Some magazines buy *First World Rights*, which means they are buying the right to run a piece for the first time in their publication and that publication has worldwide circulation. Variations of First Rights restricted to a stipulated circulation area are *First South American Serial Rights*, *First European Serial Rights*, etc.

Reprint Rights: Refers to the right to publish a work that has already been published previously. *Second Rights*, or *Second Reprint Rights*, may refer to the right to publish a piece the second time, after the purchaser of first rights has used it. There are *Second Serial Rights* and there are reprint rights not limited to serial or periodical publications, such as reprint rights sold to anthologies, collections of short work by a single author, etc.

Simultaneous Rights: Refers to the right to publish a work at the same time other publications may publish it. In other words, the writer may sell Simultaneous Rights to more than one publisher at the same time, provided the publisher buys such rights, of course. Newspapers, Sunday supplements, religious magazines, are some examples of publications that may buy such rights. The important consideration is that the circulation areas of such publications do not overlap or infringe on each other.

One-Time Rights: This phrase is sometimes used as a synonym for Simultaneous Rights and is also used to refer to the right to use a work one time, no other stipulations or restrictions involved. Photographers and illustrators often sell One-Time Rights to their material.

Syndication Rights: Refers to the right to syndicate a work, or publish it, in a newspaper syndicate whereby it will appear in a number of newspapers across the country (and in some cases, in foreign countries) simultaneously. 'Syndication Rights' most often refer to a case where a book publisher sells the rights to a syndicate to run installments of a book in one or more newspapers.

BOOK RIGHTS

Like book writing itself, the subject of book rights is much broader and more complex than magazine or periodical rights. Books have a more diverse market potential and this have more rights that may be sold. What follows is a list of rights that can be derived from the production of a book. The names of these rights should be generally self-explanatory and, with the definitions provided above concerning magazine rights, etc., the book rights list should be fairly easy to understand. 'Trade' in this context applies to books that have limited readership appeal, such as nonfiction how-to or self-help books. Bear in mind that very few books realize the sale of all the rights listed below and that every right listed does not automatically apply to every published book. The list outlines the limits of book sales potential and should offer an idea as to the amount of money that can be made from a highly successful book.

BOOK RIGHTS (rights usually dealt with in the book publisher's contract from which the book publisher oridinarily gets a percentage)

Hardcover Rights (fiction or nonfiction)

Trade Hardcover Rights (usually nonfiction)
Mass Market Paperback Rights
Trade Paperback Rights
Book Club Rights
Sequel or Next-Book Option
1st, 2nd Serial, Other Reprint Rights
Microfilm Rights
Anthology & Textbook Permissions
Condensed-Version Rights
Revised Edition Rights
Cheap & Limited Edition Rights

After making the book sale, the agent usually handles:

Dramatic Rights (film, movie, stage)
Foreign Rights
Translation Rights
Merchandising Rights
Character Rights

ANALYZING YOUR BOOK CONTRACT

The following guidelines should be used to assist the author when examining a contract that has been offered by a publisher.

It should be pointed out that the writer who has not had a book published previously is usually in a weak bargaining position. Also, s/he often is not knowledgeable about the traps and pitfalls which are found in virtually every book contract.

Most 'first-timers' are inclined to accept the statement by the publisher that "this is our standard book contract," especially when it is accompanied by a four or six-page printed document. In fact, there is no such thing as a 'standard' contract. There is, rather, a 'basic' contract which, almost without exception, has been written in such a way as to offer the maximum advantage to the publisher.

But there is nothing in the printed contract that cannot be changed. Entire paragraphs and sections may be deleted, wording of sentences can be altered, typewritten supplements may be added, etc. Whenever such changes are made, however, they must be initialed by all of the parties signing the agreement.

The Major Danger Areas

Royalties. Usually the first section of the contract an author examines is the Royalty Agreement. Too many times if the author sees '10%,' he signs the contract and sends it back. He has heard that the standard royalty is ten percent.

More and more publishers today are basing royalties on 'net receipts,' not on the retail price. What this slight change means to the author is substantial. Example: Assume a royalty of 10 percent of net receipts vs. 10 percent of retail price. If a book sells for $10.00, the royalty is $1.00 per copy, if the royalty is based on the retail price. However, the "net receipt" may be only $5.00 (if a 50% discount is given to a wholesaler), which means that the royalty would be 50 cents per copy. If your book sells 10,000 copies, you would receive only $5,000 instead of $10,000.

Our recommendations for minimum royalties (usually the best a first-time book writer can get) are:

> 10% on lst 5,000 copies
> 12 1/2% on next 5,000 copies
> 15% on all copies in excess of 10,000.
> (all based on the retail price of the book)

These percentages apply to 'trade' sales, i.e., sales of books to bookstores.

If a publisher sells a substantial number of books by mail order, the royalties are generally less than for trade sales. We recommend a minimum of five percent (of retail price). The Authors Guild suggests 18 percent of Publisher's net receipts.

Advances. The first-time book writer is in a poor bargaining position when it comes to advance payments, primarily because s/he has no track record and the publisher hesitates to put out very much front money. However, with rare exceptions (some University Presses do not pay advances), the author should insist on a minimum of $500.00. Most of the major publishers will offer more than that, but seldom more than $5,000 to a first-time author. The author must realize that such advance payments are *advances against royalties*, not an outright gift. Usually the publisher will pay 1/2 of the advance upon the signing of the contract, and 1/2 upon receipt of the completed manuscript. But read the advance clause carefully—it may state that the second half will be paid upon *publication*, which could be a year or more after you have completed the manuscript. If the publisher decides not to publish the book, it may attempt to recover the advance. The contract should state that the advance is not refundable if the author meets his/her commitments relative to manuscript delivery dates, etc.

Publication date of proposed book and manuscript delivery date. The publisher will insist on including in the contract the deadline date for delivery of a satisfactory manuscript. Be sure to allow yourself adequate time, for if you fail to deliver as stated in the contract, the publisher can void the contract and demand a refund of the advance.

It is important that the publisher state a publication date. This should be about 12 months after receipt of the completed manuscript, and in no case longer than 18 months. If the publisher doesn't indicate a time for publication, the contract actually has little meaning for the writer, since the publishing company could tie up a particular manuscript for years at no expense (other than the advance) to it.

Option clause. The best option clause is no option clause. The worst option clause is one stating that the publisher has an option to your next **work, and on the same terms as the present contract.** One of the fairest option agreements appears in this contract from David McKay Company: "The Author hereby grants to the Publishers the option to publish his next book on terms to be arranged, and shall submit the manuscript thereof to them prior to showing it to any other publisher. The Publishers shall have thirty days in which to advise the Author if they are going to exercise said option, and upon what terms." It should be noted that the author cannot offer the same book to another publisher on *better terms* than offered by the publisher holding the option.

Copyright. Under the terms of the Copyright Law now in effect (as of January 1, 1978), an author's manuscript is considered to be copyrighted from the time of creation. Unless the work is one 'done for hire' (this phrase is explained under the section, "Highlights of the Copyright Laws"), the contract should state that the work is to be copyrighted in the name of the author. Also, under the new copyright law there is no renewal of copyright, and any reference to renewal should be deleted.

Subsidiary Rights

Under the present copyright law, the Author automatically owns ALL RIGHTS unless s/he specifically assigns them to the publisher. Most publishers have indicated that their book contracts have not been changed as a result of the copyright law, since their contracts spelled out all of the rights they were purchasing, then and now. In most cases, the publisher includes the purchase of ALL RIGHTS in the contract.

If you have a literary agent who is knowledgeable and competent, s/he can often sell subsidiary rights on better terms (as far as the author is concerned) than the publisher. Therefore, those paragraphs in the contract relating to the British Commonwealth, for example, should be deleted. Likewise, translation rights should be retained by the author. If you do not have an agent, the publisher may be in a better position to sell these rights than you are, even though your share may be less than if you handled the sale yourself. In the event of an outright sale of rights made by the publisher, you should receive a *minimum* of 50 percent of the receipts, and preferably 75 percent. On books sold abroad, the publisher will usually offer 1/2 the royalty being paid on domestic sales. You should not accept less.

Movie, TV, dramatic rights. These rights, whether or not you have an agent, should be retained by the author. If your book is successful, you can negotiate the sale of the rights to television or the movies on your own (with the help of an attorney), or you may wish to retain an agent specializing in these fields. If the publisher insists on these rights, it should receive 10%.

Paperback, book club, other rights. Unless you have an agent, it is
generally better to include these rights in the contract and permit
the publisher to handle the negotiations. However, a provision
should be included in the contract requiring the publisher to obtain
your approval before selling any of these rights. You should
receive, in the event the publisher licenses a paperback house to
publish, or a book club to publish, at least 50 percent of the
income. The Authors Guild recommends a sliding scale based on
total income. (If the total income is more than $10,000, the author
should receive 60 percent. If the total income is more than $20,000,
the author should receive 70 percent).

If the publisher should issue a cheap edition, the author should
receive a minimum of 6 percent of the retail price (with step-up
increases in royalty for sales above 150,000).

Other Considerations Worth Studying

No legitimate royalty publishing house will request the author to pay for any
portion of the production or promotion costs of his/her book, nor will it require
that the author purchase copies of the book as a condition of publication.

It is acceptable practice for the publisher to charge (against the author's
royalty account) for *author's* corrections (called 'AC's') made on the galleys
that exceed 10 percent of the cost of composition.

The author usually is required to obtain all permissions for copyrighted
material being used in the book, and to pay any fees relating to these permissions.

If an index is required, it is the responsibility of the author to prepare it.
In most cases, the publisher will arrange for this to be done if the author
wishes, but it will be done at the author's expense.

Usually the publisher arranges for illustrations, if required, but this is not
always the case. In any event, who shall provide illustrations should be
spelled out in the contract.

Most contracts state that the author must deliver a manuscript that is
satisfactory to the publisher. There are occasions when a publisher attempts
to use this phrase as a method of voiding the contract. Fortunately, the courts
frequently rule in favor of the author after testimony by expert witnesses.

The author should insist that the contract provide him/her with the right
of final approval of any changes in the text. Likewise, that the title should
not be changed except by mutual consent.

If the book is a joint authorship (or a writer and photographer, writer and
illustrator, etc.), the contract should specify the percentage of royalty to be
paid to each party, and how the royalties are to be paid. If an agent is
representing both authors, the contract should state that payment is to be
made to the agent, and a statement made as to how the agent is to divide the
royalty payments.

Royalty payments. A statement of royalties due and royalty payments should be made twice a year, and within three months from the closing date of the royalty statement. The author should have the privilege of having the royalty account audited by a certified public accountant of his/her choosing (and at the author's expense).

Assignment of Agreement. Neither party shall assign the agreement, in whole or in part, without the written consent of the other.

Indemnity clause. Virtually all contracts include a 'warranty and indemnity' clause in which the author certifies that he or she is the author and that there is nothing libelous in the work. If possible, this should be qualified by adding the phrase, "to the author's knowledge." In the event of a suit brought against the publisher and/or author, the author is required to pay for the costs of defending the action, as well as damages. It is suggested that the author have inserted a statement that the publisher will pay 50 percent of such costs and/or damages that are in excess of amounts paid (or payable) to the author.

Arbitration. The contract should state that in the event of controversy that cannot be resolved by the parties, that the matter shall be submitted to the American Arbitration Association.

Some Final Words

We have touched only some of the more significant points. As mentioned previously, the beginning writer may not be able to obtain the most favorable contract, but should insist, if at all possible, on the points covered under "The Major Danger Areas."

PLAGIARISM AND PIRACY

Peculiarities Of Literary Property

Property is generally defined as something belonging to someone to the exclusion of everyone else. Though in an ideal sense 'property' should belong to the one who made or created it, in reality property can be owned through circumstances such as inheritance, discovery and first claim.

Literary property is subject to all these possible avenues of ownership but the one of creation usually prevails. Like all art forms, literature is especially recognized as belonging to its creator. The rewards of ownership can be socially and personally edifying as well as practical. Authors may enjoy esteem in the eyes of the public and may also make money from the sale of their work.

But though the creation and consequent ownership of literary property may have its diverse and satisfying rewards, such ownership also has its peculiar perils. Once a literary work is published (and sometimes even before), it is vulnerable to pilferage as no other work can be.

Though a book, an article, play or story, may be embodied within the tangible covers of a bound and printed volume, the medium in which that work is manifest, *words*, is almost as easily lifted as breathing air. As Alexander Lindsey says in his book *Plagarism and Originality*, "You cannot fence in a story or chain it down or lock it in a safe deposit box. You can copyright it, of course, and erect a NO TRESPASSING sign in the form of a copyright notice, but all that does is give you remedies against a larcenist *after* he's done his deed."

Literary property is intangible and incorporeal. It inheres neither in the printed matter nor the page on which the print appears. The *means* by which it is communicated to others is irrelevant. What is relevant, what determines ownership, is the *manner in which it is expressed*. To quote Sir William Blackstone:

"The identity of a literary composition consists entirely in the sentiment and the language: the same conceptions, clothed in the same words, must necessarily be the same composition; and whatever method be taken of exhibiting that composition to the ear or the eye of another, by recital, by writing, or by printing, in any number of copies, or at any period of time, it is always the identical work of the author which is so exhibited; and no man. . .can have a right to exhibit it, especially for profit, without the author's consent."

What belongs to the author is the unique and original way he/she has arranged such basic elements of a literary work as words, phrases, ideas, situations, characters, etc. But those elements themselves may very well belong in the public domain. The raw material, in other words, belongs to all; the way the author fashions that material into something new is totally his or her own.

Theft Of Literary Property

The terms 'plagiarism,' 'piracy,' and 'infringement' are often used interchangeably and, though they sometimes lack perfect legal precision when used in court, they have distinctions.

Infringement involves the illegal copying of a copyrighted work, or a portion of such a work, without the author or copyright owner's permission. Such copying can be an intentional case of theft or it can be unintentional (the infringer may be unaware the work is copyrighted, for example), but the infringer is, nonetheless, in violation of copyright law in either case and a court would likely decide in the claimant's favor. Both piracy and plagiarism can be an act of infringement only if the work is copyrighted.

Piracy involves the wholesale or verbatim lifting of another's work without attempting to change or disguise the original in any way and then passing the original off as the pirate's own by signing his/her name to the stolen work. The work does not have to be copyrighted. In other words, if someone took something written by Hawthorne (whose work is in the public domain) and tried to pass it off as his own work, he would be guilty of piracy.

Plagiarism is similar to piracy except that here the thief tries to disguise the actual body of the original work by writing it a bit differently or altering it in some way so as to make the public think it is the thief's original work. The element of fraud is stronger in plagiarism than in piracy. In the latter, the thief does nothing but sign his own name to another's work. In the former, the plagiarizer attempts to cover up the theft of the work by changing its character. As a result, plagiarism is the most difficult of all to prove.

Court costs and other hassles make most plagiarism cases too impractical to even try. And often the claimant suffers from a mental malady in which he/she sees too readily his/her own work in the works of others when in fact no case of theft or fraud exists. Sometimes this mental disorder on the part of the claimant is, however, a result of ignorance rather than vanity or paranoia. Many writers simply do not know or quite understand just what they can call their own and what constitutes public domain.

Words in the dictionary, historic facts and geographic places, as well as the characteristics of the human species are all considered to be public knowledge and therefore in the public domain. Likewise ideas, be they a new mathematical formula or a surgeon perfecting a technique for performing heart surgery, cannot be protected. As Philip Wittenberg states in *The Protection of Literary Property*, "All are free to use them, but the synthesis in words which the author creates is property. In that, and only that, can he claim exclusivity."

There are countless cases in legal records of claims of plagiarism wherein the claimant has accused an author of stealing his or her idea which the court ruled in favor of the defendant. Nobody owns an idea. Two authors can take the same idea and create two completely different books. If, however, that one idea were shown to have been developed and treated too similarly in both works, the implication of plagiarism would be in evidence and the originator would have a strong case against the copier.

The claimant must prove, of course, that s/he is the original author. This isn't difficult if the claimant has a copy of the original manuscript to offer as evidence, less difficult still if the original work is published. But for the claimant to accuse another writer of theft and not be able to produce recorded or tangible evidence that s/he is its creator (and there have been such cases) is unadulterated folly.

The more developed and uniquely treated a work, the more assured its creator may be of ownership insurance. A 'common' or biographical character may belong in the public domain but a strongly conceived and delineated fictive character which would be easily recognized as the creation of a particular author, belongs to him or her. The same can be said for any element in a written work so long as that element has been developed beyond the elemental stage, has taken on a unique flesh-and-blood individuality. Here is one more incentive for writers to work in the realm of the specific and concrete and to be original and fresh in the treatment of their material.

In a decision concerning a play and a movie which had similarities of situation, plot and character, the court had this to say: "Upon any work, and especially upon a play, a great number of patterns of increasing generality will fit equally well, as more and more of the incident is left out. The last may perhaps be no more than the most general statement of what the play is about, and at times might consist only of its title; but there is a point in this series of abstractions where they are no longer protected, since otherwise the playwright could prevent the use of his 'ideas,' to which, apart from their expression, his property is never extended.

"Nobody has ever been able to fix that boundary, and nobody ever can. In some cases the question has been treated as though it were analogous to lifting a portion out of the copyrighted work. . .but the analogy is not a good one, because, though the skeleton is a part of the body, it pervades and supports the whole. In such cases we are rather concerned with the line between expression and what is expressed. As respects plays, the controversy chiefly centers upon the characters and sequence of incident, these being the substance...

"If *Twelfth Night* were copyrighted, it is quite possible that a second comer might closely imitate Sir Toby Belch or Malvolio as to infringe, but it would not be enough that for one of his characters he cast a riotous knight who kept wassail to the discomfort of the household, or a vain and foppish steward who became amorous of his mistress. These would be no more than Shakespeare's 'ideas' in the play, as little capable of monopoly as Einstein's Doctrine of Relativity, or Darwin's theory of the Origin of the Species. It follows that the less developed the characters the less they can be copyrighted; that is the penalty an author must bear for marking them too indistinctly."

Just as the claimant must prove original author, s/he must also prove that the defendant in a plagiarism suit had *access* to the original work. This does not mean, however, that direct evidence must be produced. Circumstantial evidence and 'reasonable inference' more often decides the case. In other words, the fact that the two works in question are indisputably similar to the point of indicating theft is enough to prove access. This may sound like a roundabout way of saying the same thing twice but redundance and circumlocution are no strangers to legality.

Common error is another concept used to sometimes prove theft or infringement. If the original work contained errors in fact (the author had Columbus poking the Italian flag in the beach off Tierra del Fuego in 1478, for example) and the defendant's work repeats the same blunders, they serve as indisputable indicators that the defendant filched from the claimant.

LIBEL AND THE WRITER

Though the First Amendment states that "Congress shall make no law...abridging the freedom of speech, or of the press...," the writer should realize that with this guarantee of freedom comes a responsibility. Freedom of the press does not permit one person to infringe upon the rights of another, nor to defame another. The law of libel is designed to offer recourse to those who have been damaged through the written word.

The dictionary defines libel as "a written defamatory statement that conveys an unjustly unfavorable impression of another person or persons, a statement published without just cause or excuse, expressed in print or in writing, tending to expose another to public hatred, contempt, or ridicule."

Defamation of character may exist if the writer calls another person heartless, a thief, a skunk, mentally incompetent, or a liar—anything that would affect his/her reputation or affect the esteem in which s/he is held.

Even if the author believed that what was published was true, if it is found to be false and if it injures someone's reputation, the author can be sued for libel. Repeating someone else's defamatory statement can also be libelous, even if the original source is given. The writer cannot escape the possibility of libel by indicating that s/he is merely stating his/her opinion. Such statements, should they contain false information which defames another are still considered libelous and will not protect the writer from a law suit. Opinions, if based on fact, may be protected, but the writer should realize that a court may disagree as to the truth or falsity of his/her statement.

The statement "it is alleged" does not protect the writer entirely, although it does help one's case. Likewise disclaimers such as "All circumstances and characters in this novel are imaginary and do not exist in real life," cannot necessarily protect the author from being sued for libel. It is prudent for the author to change the real-life characters—their appearance, their occupation, their locale—so there is less chance of their being recognizable to others.

Should you be able to obtain a release form signed by the subject or subjects in your story in which you are given permission to write about their private lives you are on fairly safe ground.

Public figures, public officials, politicians, movie stars can be written about with less concern about defamation and invasion of privacy, providing that the statements made can be proven to be true. Even a public figure can win a lawsuit by proving that false statements were made with actual malice or reckless disregard of the truth. According to the Supreme Court, "The communications media are entitled to act on the assumption that public officials and public figures have voluntarily exposed themselves to increased risk of injury from defamatory falsehoods concerning them. No such assumption is justified with respect to a private individual."

Perhaps even a greater danger for a writer is being sued for the invasion of privacy. Although truth is generally considered to be the best defense in the case of a libel action, an author can lose a law suit even if the truth is on his/her side—if his/her words constitute the invasion of a private person's rights.

Only the person who has been defamed can sue for libel(relatives, friends, descendants do not have any rights). Therefore the author is in little danger if writing about a dead person, although a few states do have a law against defaming the dead.

One way to reduce the chances of libel is to state facts and allow the readers to draw their own conclusions. For example, instead of stating that Mr. Doe is incompetent or dishonest, describe the circumstances that will lead the readers to that assumption. Avoid making a definite statement that someone is mentally or physically incompetent or guilty of a crime unless you can back up that statement.

There are no positive safeguards that will insure the writer against the possibility of a lawsuit. Some suggestions to help you avoid a libel suit:

1. Avoid statements (true or false) that could be considered defamatory.
2. Verify your facts.
3. Avoid malice.
4. Disguise your characters so that identification will be impossible or at least improbable.

USING A PEN NAME

There haven't been many cases of someone stealing a well-known author's by-line and trying to pass it off as his or her own in order to sell a manuscript but it has happened. A famous name can be a piece of property as well as a created work and sometimes writers dream up a *nom de plume* for the sole purpose of trying to embellish or improve their publishability. 'Mark Twain' no doubt sounded much better (and had a significant relevance to his interest in the Mississippi) than his given name, Sam Langhorne Clemens. He also may have convinced himself that his Mississippi riverboat monicker would gain him a wider readership.

Perhaps it did but, nine times out of ten, the name below a written work's title has no influence on either an editor or the public. What both want is a good piece of writing that starts below that by-line and ends with the work's last page.

There are, nonetheless, a few good reasons for conjuring up a literary alias. George Sand (aka Amandine-Aurore-Lucile Dudevant) had two good reasons. Her real name was a jawbreaker, maybe even to the French, and she was a woman writing when women just did not do such things. Undoubtedly Aurore Dudevant would have had a hard time getting published under her true name.

Nowadays a querulous male writer might complain that the pendulum has swung the other way and, if he wants acceptance, writing under a feminine by-line could well help his chances of making a sale. Be that as it may, if he wants to write for a woman's magazine which prefers its readers to think it accepts material written only by women, he'll need a better by-line than Bruno Rake, say. The same applies to a woman writing for a men's magazine that wants only masculine by-lines for their stories.

Some other valid reasons for using a pen name could occur when you have more than one article in a single issue of a magazine, or you're having a lot of titles coming out in a short period of time, and so forth. (Such creative outpouring should happen to us all.)

The procedure when using a pseudonym is simple. Type your legal name in the upper left-hand corner of the manuscript and your pen name under the title. This tells the editor to publish the material under your by-line but that your check-in-payment should be made out to the name indicated in the upper left-hand corner.

It's a good idea to avoid using an odd, obscure or fancy name. Use a given name, not initials. If you are selling frequently under a pen name, advise an officer at your bank to make a record of your professional name. A checking account may be set up in both names. Also inform the Post Office; your mail may be damned to the Limbo of the Undeliverable otherwise.

When signing a book contract, use your legal name, but include in the contract the name under which the book is to be published. If your pen name is not a part of the agreement, the publisher is not required to use it.

If the copyright notice is shown with your pen name (which it normally should be), you will have to indicate both your legal name and pen name of the Application for Copyright.

Alternate Book Publishing

For the author seeking a publisher, there are various categories of subsidy publishers, vanity publishers and printers who specialize in book manufacture.

Some subsidy publishers serve a legitimate function, publishing certain technical and special interest books that deserve publication but are so limited in appeal that they cannot be published for a profit.

The vanity publishers make a pretense of being legitimate publishers, offering royalties, a promotional program, sending books to reviewers, etc., and generally implying to authors that they will recover their investment through the royalties they receive. The cost to the author is usually about double what s/he would pay to have the same book printed by a book printer and rarely is the implied profit even remotely realized.

Book printers make no pretense about sales or distribution. They quote the author a price for so many books and deliver the books to the author. It probably cannot be emphasized enough that for those who cannot obtain a satisfactory contract with a royalty publisher and have the funds to publish their own book, this is the most practical path to take.

I. SUBSIDY PUBLISHING

The Vanity Presses

For some years, straight vanity publishing has existed. Disappointed and frustrated writers, often of immature or little ability and unable to interest a royalty publisher in their work, have paid these so-called publishers to issue their books. With few exceptions, the only result was such satisfaction as the writer derived from having a copy of his/her book to give to friends.

In recent years, vanity publishing has reached out for respectability by offering services other than merely printing a book. However, it should be understood that 'subsidy' or 'cooperative' publishing (as the contemporary vanity publishers prefer to label it) offers the writer no more than what s/he pays for.

Even in some of the vanity publishers' own literature, they will tell you not to go the subsidy route if you expect to make money from your book. According to Nelson Richardson, former staff writer for *Coda: Poets & Writers Newsletter*, "Sales rarely occur, except for a few copies purchased by friends." And most vanity publishers will admit that "only 10% of their authors get their investment back from sales. It's not unusual for a vanity book to sell less than 25 copies."

A point that should be stressed is that the vanity house has little or no incentive for seeing that a book sells; the vanity house makes its money directly from the author, often before the book is galleyed, and if delays or other problems arise, more charges will often result—and, as will be shown in some woeful cases reported by writers, the author may still, after having paid thousands, not see his or her book in print.

Claims or promises in vanity literature that the book will be reviewed, promoted, etc., stretch the truth to the breaking point. Reviewers, as a rule, will not look at a vanity title, librarians refuse to take them seriously and bookstore buyers, upon seeing vanity imprints, will tell you they want nothing to do with them. What little promotion or reviewing is done, if it can be called that, comes usually from the vanity publisher's staff and is done in the most cursory fashion, just enough to stay legally within the ad promises and contractual guarantees. "Vanity imprints are treated the same way vanity press editors treat their manuscripts," says Nelson Richardson,"—with indifference."

Subsidy publishers do not employ salesmen to call on bookstores. The widespread publicity, the autographing parties, TV and other interviews, second editions, movie, TV and dramatic rights, paperback and foreign rights that the vanity ads would lead you to believe are probable, if not certain, eventualities, should be seen as pure hype. The vanity contract guarantees none of these things and the vanity imprint militates against their ever being achieved.

What the writer does receive from the vanity publisher generally consists of: a somewhat professionally printed book, a mediocre dust jacket, some (very little) editing, a stock mailing piece sent to a list of names provided by the writer, inclusion of his title in a catalogue, the copyright of his book, billing, bookkeeping and handling by the publisher and a limited number of review copies sent out to newspapers and/or magazines which are usually ignored. Some vanity presses fail to deliver even these services.

Some Experiences With Vanity Publishers

While a few writers who have run the risk of publishing with a vanity press and, largely through their own promotional and distributional efforts, have seen their work sell enough to cover the cost, the overwhelming number who have chosen this course have ended up outraged and fleeced. A few summarized cases should illustrate the kinds of dilemmas incurred when dealing with a vanity house.

The major vanity houses may print as many as 700 titles a year, and the complaints may easily run into the hundreds. After a writer in Oklahoma paid one of these so-called publishers $5,000.00, his manuscript was held for more than a year before it was published; no publicity or promotion was done and the illustrations were poor quality black and white. The book sold less than 50 copies and when the author complained the publisher declared the book a "poor mover" and suggested cancelling the contract.

A California writer paid this same publisher $6,046.00. The book's delay in publication was blamed on the author when the vanity press requested she revise the galley proofs. The mistakes in the galleys were, according to the writer, the publisher's. Even the *revised* proofs had errors. After returning the proofs, along with another check (for "extra charges"), the author heard nothing for months. Inquiries went unanswered.

A North Dakota writer paid a vanity press $9,000.00, misled by their carefully worded advertising and the likewise carefully worded contract (concealing more than it revealed) into thinking that at least 4000 copies of the book would be printed. His "royalties" amounted to less than $150.00 and he received 50 books. When a friend of his ordered copies of the book from the publisher before the expiration of the contract, he got no response. The author lost 92% of his investment.

Edward Uhlan, retired president and founder of Exposition Press(one of the larger vanity presses) had this to say: "Contemporary subsidy publishing was conceived in sin and dedicated to fraud." And: "Much of the censure that subsidy publishing has been subjected to has been justified, in my opinion, and is mainly due to the built-in larceny of the contract itself."

Semi-subsidy Publishers

Some publishers publish both royalty and subsidy books, though they keep quiet about the latter and, in most cases, serve a legitimate and worthwhile purpose in bringing them out. Without the blandishments and flattery heaped on the writer by the vanity publisher, without claiming or implying that the author will enjoy wealth and fame from the publication of his or her book, semi-subsidy or legitimate subsidy publisher will pay a certain percentage of the book's cost and require the author to pay the rest; often, however, the author pays the full cost. These houses usually publish under subsidy contract such books as biographies, technical works, stories of politicians, businessmen and corporations and industrial history. University presses are in this group and often agree to do a subsidy book when it is of excellent scientific or scholarly value, the kind of book that would have small chance of paying for itself through regular sales.

II. BOOK CO-OPS

A writers' cooperative consists of a group of writers who want total control of all areas of production and distribution of their work, who are fed up with the stumbling blocks of the commercial market and are willing to contribute both money and labor in order to see that their work remains, in every sense, theirs. Like any other co-op, expenses and labor are shared and in this sharing, costs in both time and money are significantly reduced.

There aren't many of these intrepid groups in the U.S. but the ones in existence are at least keeping their heads above water and seem to think the enterprise worth the toil and tears. Grants often help support them and sales are made more often than not by the members getting out and hustling on their own. Readings, advertising locally and through the mail are some of the usual methods of promotion. Distribution is accomplished by professional distributors the co-op hires or again through the use of the mail, local fairs and bookstores.

Reviews of co-op books often appear in such publications as *Home Grown Books Librarians' Browser, Small Press, Library Journal, Small Press Review* and others. Financially successful writers and other literary patrons sometimes contribute money and encouragement. With the exception of The Fiction Collective, all are primarily composed of poets and concern themselves basically with regional or local audiences. Some co-ops may require an initiation fee. Books are sometimes financed solely by the author but often the author's money is helped by proceeds from previous books and other co-op money. Most will accept new members; write an inquiry if interested in joining one. Or, if interested in starting your own co-op, those who have already blazed the trail might offer helpful advice.

III. SELF-PUBLISHING

While publication by a vanity press invites disrepute, self-publishing suffers no such stigma. James Joyce, Thomas Paine, Mark Twain, Walt Whitman and Hart Crane are some of those who ventured into this exacting enterprise at one time or another in their careers. As recent a best seller as Robert Ringer's *Winning Through Intimidation* was self-published initially, so the tradition is alive and well.

But self-publishing is in no way to be confused with vanity publishing and the use of such names as those mentioned above in vanity press ads is a good example of the kinds of factual distortions resorted to by such publishers. In self-publishing the author takes on the entire task himself, and it is a task requiring faith, fortitude and energy. Final preparation of the manuscript, copyediting, design, typesetting, proofreading, manufacturing, registering copyright, publicity, advertising, sales and distribution all must be carried out. Every one of these jobs can be hired in whole or in part but large expenses may, of course, result.

The easiest mode of operation is to work with a printer or book manufacturer who will help you transform the manuscript into a bound book. The most expensive and complicated method is to freelance separately the tasks involved, the author acting, more or less, as his/her own managing editor. High quality will be realized but you will have paid the price. The least expensive method is to work with a local printer who will provide advice and aid; but in this case you will be basically on your own.

Promotion, distribution and marketing will be the hardest jobs and the publications listed below contain useful information concerning these areas. There are book promoters who will aid in publicizing and selling a book, either through a direct-mail campaign or display advertising. It is possible, too, to employ someone or a firm to handle the wrapping and mailing of orders of your book. Distribution can be achieved through placing coupon ads in newspapers and magazines or renting mailing lists of likely customers. If a mail-order ad generates sufficient interest, you will have a better chance of interesting a distributor. Also, you can contact retail booksellers in your area and persuade them to stock your book. A bookseller usually is allowed to purchase the book at a 40% discount.

Some Useful Publications for Self-Publishers

Books (obtainable through bookstores or by order to publisher):

- *The Self-Publishing Manual*, by Dan Poynter, Parachute Publications, PO Box 4232, Santa Barbara, CA 93103.
- *How to Self-Publish Your Own Book and Make It a Best Seller*, by Ted Nicholas. Enterprise Publishing Co., 1300 Market St., Wilmington, DE 19801.
- *The Publish-It-Yourself Handbook* Pushcart Press's Rev. Ed., edited by Bill Henderson. Pushcart Press, PO Box 380, Wainscott, NY 11975.
- *How to Publish, Promote, and Sell Your Book*, by Joseph Goodman, Adams Press, 30 W. Washington St., Chicago, IL 60602.
- *The Writer-Publisher*, by Charles N. Aronson. Charles N. Aronson Writer Publisher, Rt. 1, Hundred Acres, Arcade, NY 14009.
- *Publish It Yourself*, by Charles Chickadel, Trinity Press, Box 1320, San Francisco, CA 94101.
- *How to Publish Your Book*, by L.W. Mueller, Harlo Press, 30 W. 16721 Hamilton Ave., Detroit, MI 48203.

Periodicals:

- *Publisher's Weekly*, R. R. Bowker, 205 E. 42nd St. New York, NY 10017.
- *Small Press*, R. R. Bowker Co., 205 E. 42nd St., New York, NY 10017.
- *Small Press Review*, PO Box 100, Paradise, CA 95969.
- *ALPS*, San Francisco Arts & Letters Foundation, POB 99394, San Francisco, CA 94109.

- *Home Grown Books Librarians' Browser*, 300 Barclay Rd., Chapel Hill, NC 27514.
- *Stony Hills*, Weeks Mills, New Sharon, ME 04955.

Some promotion and distribution sources:

- *American Book Trade Directory* (available in reference libraries). R. R. Bowker, 205 E. 42nd St. New York, NY 10017. Names and addresses of 12,000 retail book outlets, categorized by specialty.
- *American Library Directory* (available in reference libraries). R. R. Bowker, 205 E. 42nd St. New York, NY 10017. Names and addresses of 30,000 libraries.
- *Literary Market Place* (available in reference libraries). R. R. Bowker, 205 E. 42nd St. New York, NY 10017.

Newsletters:

- *COSMEP Newsletter*, PO Box 703, San Francisco, CA 94101
- *Writer's Newsletter*, 316 N. Jordan, Bloomington, IN 47405
- *Newsletter*, Long Island Poetry Collective, Inc., PO Box 773, Huntington, NY 11743
- *The Public Press Newsletter*, 423 W. 46th St., New York, NY 10036

As said before, many, if not all, of those "famous authors who published their first book themselves," did not go to a vanity or subsidy publisher to do so but dealt directly with a printer. If you have your book printed, you buy and pay for the entire edition. You may select your choice of book paper, kind and size of type, and design your own format. When the book is printed it is shipped and delivered to you. You have all the books, but they become your responsibility. There is nothing difficult or complicated about obtaining copyright, listing in *Publisher's Weekly* or sending out review copies. A little systematic bookkeeping simplifies record keeping. You need no special license to sell your own book. In some states you may have to obtain a sales-tax permit covering sales of the book within your state.

The cost of printing as compared with subsidy publishing may vary greatly. Several small printers issue editions of 100 or more copies, if they do not run more than 100-150 pages. Extra services also may be available at a cost. If you can do your own publicity, selling and bookkeeping, the cost of your edition can be, of course, greatly reduced.

Printers and binders are listed in the Yellow Pages or in *Literary Market Place*. You should obtain estimates from a number of competing firms, and samples of their work as well as information on their production methods and schedules.

Glossary

ADVANCE. Money paid to author before book publication.

CAPTION. Identification or description of a photograph.

CONTRIBUTOR COPIES. Issues of a magazine sent to an author in which his/her work appears.

COPY EDITING. Editing for punctuation, grammar and consistency of style.

COPYRIGHT. A means to protect a writer's work and show ownership.

DISK. Used in a word processor to store data.

DOT MATRIX. Printer type which forms letters with tiny dots.

EL-HI. Elementary to high school, also simple vocabulary text with teenage appeal.

FAIR USE. The use of short passages from copyrighted work without infringing on the owner's rights.

GHOSTWRITER. A writer who writes for and in the name of another.

GRAPHICS. Photographs, drawings, artwork or other illustrations.

INVASION OF PRIVACY. Possible cause for suits against a writer who has written about somebody without their consent.

KILL FEE. Partial payment made to a writer when an assigned article is not published.

LETTER QUALITY. Printer that produces typewriter quality letters.

LIBEL. A published statement which exposes a person to ridicule, contempt, loss of reputation, business or property.

MULTIPLE MANUSCRIPT SUBMISSION. Sending a manuscript to more than one publication at the same time.

MASS MARKET. The public at large.

MODEL RELEASE. A paper signed by the subject giving the photographer permission to use the photograph.

PAYMENT ON ACCEPTANCE. Payment is made to the writer as soon as the editor accepts the manuscript.

PAYMENT ON PUBLICATION. Payment is made when the article, story or poem is published.

PEN NAME. Pseudonym used instead of your actual name on manuscripts.

PLAGIARISM. Taking another's writing and passing it off as your own.

PUBLIC DOMAIN. Printed material which was never copyrighted or whose copyright has terminated.

QUERY. A brief, informative letter outlining an article which might be of interest to an editor.

ROYALTIES. Percentage paid to the author from book sales.

SASE. Self-addressed stamped envelope.

SCREENPLAY. A play meant to be seen in motion picture theatres.

SIDEBAR. Supplemental information accompanying a feature article.

SLANT. Writing the article or story to match the style or interests of a magazine.

SPECULATION. An editor agreeing to read a manuscript with no guarantee that it will be accepted.

SUBSIDIARY RIGHTS. Additional rights sold after 1st publication.

SUBSIDY PUBLISHER. A publisher who charges the author for the cost of producing a book.

SYNOPSIS. A summary of a book.

TELEPLAY. A play written for television.

TREATMENT. Summary of a television or film script.

Index

A

adult magazine markets 74, 75
advances 132
anecdote markets 89-92
articles, types of 43
article markets 55-57
article writing 43
article writing, references 43
associations directory 99
associations, use of 19, 20
authors, reference 15
Ayer's Directory of Newspapers 97

B

bookkeeping 109-110
bookkeeping, double entry 110
bookkeeping, single entry 110
Books in Print 15, 23
book club rights 134
book contracts 131-135
book market opportunities 57, 58
book reviews, writing 41, 42
book reviews, writing, refs. 42
book rights 129, 130
business of writing 103-108

C

cameras 5
card catalog 20-23
characterization 31
character defamation 140, 141
children's book markets 64-67
children's book markets, ref. 67
column writing 40
column writing, references 40
computers 4
computer reference books 14
confession magazine market 77-79
contracts, book 131-135
copyright 117-125
copyright duration 118
copyright forms 123
copyright infringement 136-139
Copyright Office 121-124
copyright ownership 119, 120
copyright reference books 14
copyright registration 120-123
criticism, manuscript 30-33

D

deductible expenses 114-115
description, style 31
detective market opportunities 71-73
Dewey Decimal System 20, 21
dictionaries 8, 9
disclaimers 140
dot matrix printers 4, 5
dramatic rights 133

E

editorial services 45
Editor and Publisher Yearbook 19

educational theatre 84-86
encyclopedias 10
expenses, deductible 114-115
expense record 112

F

fair use doctrine 124
fantasy market opportunities 68-70
fiction market 54, 55
fiction, criticism 30-32
filler markets 89-92
foreign rights 128

G

government, use of 19
grammar 12, 13

H

house organ markets 57
humor markets 89-92

I

ideas, finding them 51, 52
income record 111
income tax for the writer 114-116
indemnity clause 135
information networks 19
infringement, copyright 136-139
inspirational book,
    magazine market 81-83
inspirational magazine markets 56
interviews, conducting 20
International Directory of
    Small Presses 98
International Literary Market Place 96
International Writers &
    Artists Yearbook 98
investment tax credit 114-115
in-flight magazine market 75

J

jokes markets 89-92
juvenile book markets 64-67

L

laser printers 5
legal information 117-125
legal reference books 14
letter quality printers 4, 5
libel 140, 141
libraries, use of 20-23
library directories 18
Literary Market Place 96
literary property 136-139
literary rights 126-130

M

magazine markets, general 55
manuscript log 113
manuscript preparation 46-50
manuscript, criticism 30-33
markets, evaluation of 54-60

market directories   96-99
men's magazine markets   74, 75
movies, as a market   59
movie rights   133
mystery market opportunities   71-73

N
National Trade Associations
   Directory   99
newspaper directories   97, 98
nom de plume   142, 143
nonfiction, criticism   32, 33
North American serial rights   128
novel writing   34-36
novel writing, references   36

O
one-time rights   129
opinion article market   55, 56
option clause   132-133

P
paperback rights   134
pay schedule for writers   104-108
pen name   142, 143
periodical indexes   10
piracy   137
plagiarism   137-139
play market opportunities   59, 60
plots, summary   15
plot development   30
plot, importance of   30, 31
poetry, criticism   44
poetry markets   57
poetry references   13, 14, 44
Poole's Index   10
proofreading   49, 50
pseudonym   142, 143
publishing, royalty book   61, 62
publishing, self   147-149
publishing, subsidy   144-146
publishing, vanity   144-146
puzzle markets   89-92

Q
query letter, how to write   100-102
quotation references   12

R
radio as a market   59
Reader's Guide to
   Periodical Literature   10, 11, 23, 28
record-keeping   109-113
reference books   12, 16
rejections, reasons for   62
religious book, magazine market   81-83
religious magazine markets   56
Religious Writer's Marketplace   99
reprint rights   128-129
research, books, articles   32, 33
research, general   17-23

research sources   18, 19
rewriting, procedure   29
rights, book club   133
rights, dramatic   133
rights, foreign   128
rights, literary   126, 130
rights, movie   133
rights, paperback   134
royalties   131, 135

S
science fiction opportunities   68-70
scriptwriting   38, 39
scriptwriting, references   39
self publishing   147-149
self-syndication   93-95
serial rights   127, 128
short story writing   37
short story writing, references   37
song market opportunities   60
sports magazine opportunities   74, 75
Standard Periodical Directory   97
Standard Rate & Data   97
style, importance of   31
subsidiary rights   133-134
subsidy publishing   144-146
syndication rights   129
syndication   93-95
synonym references   13

T
tape recorders   6
taxes, income   114-115
taxpayer bill of rights   116
television market opportunities   58, 59
television rights   133
television writing   38, 39
trade magazine markets   57
travel expenses   114-115
travel magazine market   75
true crime market opportunities   72, 73
typewriters   4

U
Ulrich's Periodicals Directory   98

V
vanity publishing   144-146

W
women's magazine market   75-79
word processing   4
work-for-hire   119
Writers' & Artists' Year Book   98
Writer's Handbook   97
Writer's Market   96
writing, technique   27-29

Y
young adult book markets   64-67
youth theatre, writing for   87, 88